CW00731738

# Praise

'The advertising industry's best stories tend to highlight the mavericks who did it their own way, made some mistakes, created great work and had a blast doing it. Go ahead and add *Brand Warfare* to this list.'

— **Mark Ronquillo**, Professor of Practise/ Advertising, Penn State Donald P. Bellisario College of Communications, and former Saatchi/Publicis/McCann/BBDO

'Not many branding books start with fights on the footy terraces, but Julian's branding and business career has been anything but conventional. His story is compelling and beautifully written (for a screen printer!), and Julian skilfully weaves his thoughts and opinions together with real-world anecdotes about the business and brand success he's created. *Brand Warfare* will have you laughing, learning and loving the power of brands.'

— **Richard Draycott**, Deputy Editor, *The Drum*

# BRAND

FROM THE TERRACES TO THE BOARDROOM

# WARFARE

## JULIAN KYNASTON

# R<sup>e</sup>think

First published in Great Britain in 2025
by Rethink Press (www.rethinkpress.com)

© Copyright Julian Kynaston

All rights reserved. No part of this publication may be reproduced, stored in or introduced into a retrieval system, or transmitted, in any form, or by any means (electronic, mechanical, photocopying, recording or otherwise) without the prior written permission of the publisher.

The right of Julian Kynaston to be identified as the author of this work has been asserted by him in accordance with the Copyright, Designs and Patents Act 1988.

This book is sold subject to the condition that it shall not, by way of trade or otherwise, be lent, resold, hired out, or otherwise circulated without the publisher's prior consent in any form of binding or cover other than that in which it is published and without a similar condition including this condition being imposed on the subsequent purchaser.

Cover design: Lee Bennett

Cover photography: (top) © John Ingledew, (bottom) © iStock/Dmitiy Jigarin

# Contents

Introduction: What Is Brand?                         1

1  Finding My Tribe                                   7
   An unlikely epiphany:
   Barnsley vs Leeds United                          10
   Who the fuck are they?                            11
   A new suit of armour                              14

2  Bound By Brands                                   19
   Fashion funds                                     19
   Birds of a feather – the NCL                      22
   Loyalty to the cause                              26
   Initiation                                        27
   Casual battles                                    29
   Casual alliances                                  32
   An unexpected escalation                          35
   A culture change                                  36
   Back to Barnsley                                  38

**3 Becoming Respectable**      **41**

Making my exit      42

Dave Ellis – a legend round the corner      45

Seeds taking root      49

Build it and they will come      50

**4 A New Kind Of Warfare**      **53**

Into the lion's den      55

Taking clients into battle      59

Logic doesn't rule      61

**5 Gaining Gravitas – Conquering The Boardroom**      **65**

You can lead a horse to water…      68

A partner in battle      75

Knowledge before assumption      78

Embracing planning – acting with conviction      82

Brand is business, business is brand      86

How do you rate an agency?      89

**6 Quality Over Quantity**      **91**

A team of calibre      92

No room for average      94

Look deeper      99

The price of average      102

**7 Kingmaking**      **105**

ghd – a blueprint for brand building      106

You can't put a price on principles 114

A brand of our own – Illamasqua 117

From truckers to retail enablers –
Clipper Logistics 126

**8 Polish It Brightly** **133**

The Sophie Lancaster Foundation 135

A lasting legacy 137

**9 GenM – Much More Than A Business** **139**

A light in the dark – and a plan 141

A radical change in approach 144

Driven by a powerhouse 146

Setting an example – a beacon of light
for other brands 148

The human cost of failing to understand
menopause – Linda and David Salmon's
story 151

An MCA award winner for social impact 153

**10 Visceralisation** **155**

How to define brand 155

Become the customer 158

**Epilogue: Life Equips You** **161**

**Appendix: Awards** **173**

**Acknowledgements** **175**

**The Author** **177**

# Introduction:
# What Is Brand?

**W**ho the fuck are they? These are the words that best describe the feeling that ran through every cell of my body the first time I saw Leeds United Football Club's notorious firm of hooligans, the Very Young Team (VYT), at Barnsley's Oakwell Stadium.

Among the sea of sombre colours in the stands, which I was a part of, one small section stood out like an oasis in a desert – a pronounced burst of bright, exciting fluorescence. These guys were donning a range of expensive brands in an array of electric colours – sky blue, yellow, white, even pink!

Putting aside the occasional game my dad had taken me to when I was too young to fully absorb the experience, I'd never been to a football match before. But when I saw that arresting display of bright tones and felt the energy coming from that group of lads, I sensed a calling. Fuck the game! Whoever or whatever this lot were, I wanted to be a part of it.

Two pitch invasions showed me how dangerous these youths were, and almost put me off, but when have humans ever let danger, or even a sense of right and wrong, get in the way of doing what they want or going with their hearts? They were free, they were expressive, they were anarchic, and they were the most exciting people I had ever seen. Overnight, I went from being a hardcore goth, who mostly dressed in black, to wanting to bleach my jeans. As well as bleached jeans, 'casuals' (a football culture associated with hooliganism and designer clothes, also known as 'firms' and 'dressers') wore Adidas or Nike trainers, bright tracksuit tops, polo shirts or Pringle sweaters. All my black stuff had to be either bleached and dyed or donated to the charity shops.

No matter what kind of a start we have in life, we all begin not having a clue who we are and where we're going. Some people could be born in the ruins of a war zone and still become billionaires. Others could be raised with a silver spoon in their mouths and amount to nothing. Many are born average and remain so, seeking comfort and finding it in anonymity, a few pints every Friday and Saturday night, a family and a job they don't hate too much. Some don't even need that much. And I'm not judging any of them. This isn't a rags-to-riches story or a motivational book on how to live a great life.

The thing that everyone has in common, regardless of the path they take, is their quest to find an identity that feels right for them. Whatever you do today, whatever you read, whatever you think, say, like or don't like will be linked in some way to your sense of identity. It is at the core of who we are. Some people struggle to find it, ever. For every human on earth, there will have been a time when the only thing that mattered was whether they were hungry, thirsty, too hot or cold, or if they needed to sleep. Then, for most of us, starting before the age of ten and gaining strength steadily as we enter our teens, we have the urge to discover ourselves and find out where we belong. One way that this plays out for many is in their taste in fashion – mods or rockers, heavy metal, goth or new romantic, punk or pop. Everyone wants to find their tribe. For me, I found it in the casuals.

But this isn't a book about football hooliganism. It is a part of my history, and I see it for what it is. There are several reasons why that chapter of my life is relevant to the themes covered in the pages to follow. One is the power of connection. Whoever I was then, almost four decades ago, and whatever was going on at the core of my being – angst, the desire to belong and to be part of something, anger, frustration, you name it – they, the VYT, were expressing it. They were living it. I felt an instant connection with them. I identified with their *brand*.

For casuals, the brand names they so proudly displayed on everything they wore were so much more than fashion accessories. They carried those labels like shields. Wearing the gear was like donning a uniform. Once we were kitted out in our loud casual clothes, we were ready to go to war and ready to stand shoulder-to-shoulder with our comrades. Put on a pair of Adidas trainers or a Fila polo shirt, and you were as hard as nails. Stick on some Armani, and you were fucking invincible!

It is over thirty years since I got out of the world of football violence and focused my energy on something constructive. Instead of insecure young men with pent-up anger and frustration and a longing to fight, my tribe – at least professionally – are the people I work with and, more importantly, the companies we serve.

Loyalty has always been one of my key strengths and a trait that I am proud to hold dear. When I work with a client to help them launch, build, strengthen or heal their brand, I hold their hand as a seasoned warrior in a battle to achieve their objectives. Part of the process is helping them to see and understand the heart and soul of their brand, what makes it tick, and to identify its tribe – the people whose needs it serves, its ideal customers.

Why am I writing this now? If it were about creating publicity for my consultancy, Propaganda, or strengthening my personal brand, I'd be more than a little late to the party. By the time this book is published, Propaganda will be thirty-three years old, and I will be coming out the other side of my mid-fifties. That said, hitting thirty is as good a reason as any to celebrate the longevity and success of the consultancy, but it's also a cause to reflect on who we are, what we believe in and why what we do is so important.

Is *Brand Warfare* a memoir? I can't share something that has meant as much to me as Propaganda and the projects we have had the honour to have been involved in without putting a lot of me in there too. From that perspective, yes, it is a memoir of sorts. Is it a how-to textbook on branding? If you're looking for a step-by-step instruction manual that you can apply to every situation, this isn't it. Besides, there are so many aspects to what we do that can't be wrapped up in an academic style text or course. I launched Propaganda having never graduated from college. What you will find here is much, much more valuable than a textbook.

In this book, I share some of Propaganda's key milestones, notable projects, lessons learned and insights discovered. The reason I've been in this industry for three decades and have no intention of quitting is that I'm as passionate about it today as I've ever been. In answering one key question, and doing that thoroughly,

I hope to give you something much more powerful than a set of commandments. That question is:

*What is brand?*

# ONE

# Finding My Tribe

The bus from Lindley to Huddersfield was heaving with people making their way home from work, and still more were getting on. There was a girl in her twenties wearing a ton of makeup and a Bananarama-inspired hairstyle, a bloke in a flat cap and donkey jacket who looked as though he might have just got out of prison, two pensioners, and a young mum with a massive brolly, a pram, and an older child.

It was a typical, cold, dark, winter evening, and it was chucking it down outside. People were fighting each other to escape the elements. But no matter how crowded that bus would get, I could bank on one thing: no one was going to take the seat next to me, not even the grubby, hairy-arsed, middle-aged man standing a couple of feet away, who was shamelessly staring at the Page Three girl in his copy of *The Sun* in full view of the rest of the bus.

That was one of the advantages of being a screen printer in the early eighties – you were guaranteed a seat to yourself on the bus. The chemicals from the ink would get into my hair, onto my skin, and into the fabric of my clothes. Every inch of me was contaminated, and the nauseating smell of my trade followed me around like a bad penny. Other travellers must have wondered if I was running a meth lab.

Other than being able to sprawl out on the bus, working in the print industry came with no other obvious perks. I was part of Thatcher's youth, working for next to nothing on a youth training scheme (YTS) in a kind of day-release setup that meant I could stay on at school to try to get a better result for art. By the time I had paid Mum for board and my nan the money I invariably owed her, I was left with a fiver for everything else, which inevitably led to another loan. My nan was my sixteen-year-old self's equivalent of the payday lender, without the extortionate interest rates.

As a trainee, I was expected to learn the trade from the ground up – quite literally in my case, as brushing the floor was one of my regular tasks. Think Mr Miyagi's 'wax on, wax off' and 'paint the fence'.[1] Somehow, I was

---

1.  JG Avildsen, *Karate Kid* (Delphi II Productions and Jerry Weintraub Productions, 1984)

supposed to become a black belt in screen printing by absorbing the ambience of the place while carefully sweeping in the prescribed manner. I was bloody good at it though. Such was my enthusiasm and attention to detail that even now, I can't walk past anything on the floor without picking it up and putting it in a bin, and I expect anyone who wants to work for me to do the same – that was the first item on my steadily growing list of employment criteria that has served me well, right up to the present day.

Before starting the YTS, I had graduated to the sixth form at Shelley High School in West Yorkshire where I chose to study art and design – I had an eye on a career in advertising and design. I say 'graduated', but I only had one O level to my name, in geography, and I was anything but an academic. Yet sixth form was a given for anyone who wanted it back then.

I was enjoying my time in sixth form, and everything was going well. At least, it was until I was gripped by an all-encompassing urge to buy bright pink jumpers with designer labels, and the money had to come from somewhere. *Bright pink jumpers? Well, it was the eighties,* you may be thinking. Yeah, it was the eighties, but I was a fully-fledged punk-cum-goth type, and prior to now had embraced the Henry Ford dress code: any colour at all, as long it was black.

All my clothes were black, and if I saw something I liked that wasn't black, I'd dye it. Those who remember me from my school days might describe me as a tall skinny guy who used to dress in black and lean against the wall, something I vaguely remember doing in an attempt to look cool. Black captured my mood perfectly and said everything I wanted to say. Black was my colour... until it wasn't.

## An unlikely epiphany: Barnsley vs Leeds United

In 1983 I'd never been into football, had no allegiance to any team and hadn't even been to a game – although I remember wanting a Leeds strip while in middle school because everyone else had Barnsley or Huddersfield kits, and I wanted to be different. But one of my friends, Ian Dickinson, persuaded me to go to a game with him. He offered to buy me a ticket for a match at Barnsley's Oakwell Stadium, where the club has been based since its formation in 1887. He wouldn't usually set foot in the place, but his beloved Leeds United were playing and he managed to rope me in, assuring me it was going to be an exciting match.

Most football fans weren't particularly adventurous dressers. Thick coats in black, brown, and other dark colours were the order of the day, with the team's scarf wrapped around the wrist for support. On the morning of the game, I was buzzing with nervous excitement and went for a full-on aggressive black look with Doc

Martens, tight black jeans and a Crombie. I looked the bollocks.

I had been so uninterested in football that I had rarely even watched it on television, but I don't think anything on a screen could have prepared me for the atmosphere of being at a live game. That's where the transformation happens, where football fans find some truth in Bill Shankly's famous assertion that football is more important than life and death. That's where supporters become lifelong fans. Others can't understand their fanaticism, perhaps because they have never been to a game and experienced the intensely tribalistic feel of it, while die-hard fans couldn't imagine life without the beautiful game.

## Who the fuck are they?

The Leeds players were in control from the first whistle, much to Ian's delight, and they'd also brought an energetic army of gregarious fans with them. A combination of rhythmic clapping and chants of 'Leeds' was belted out periodically by the people on our side of the pitch for the duration of the game. I was surrounded by noise, not least from Ian.

Occasionally, the home supporters tried to drum up a bit of enthusiasm for their players with lacklustre renditions of 'Oh when the Reds go marching in,' but they weren't convincing anyone. Their choice of song seemed a little bizarre, given that their team was getting thrashed and would most likely be retreating from the pitch dejectedly rather than marching anywhere (Leeds did in fact bag a two–nil victory). I am struck by an amusing sense of irony while writing this as, these days, I am a loyal Barnsley fan and have been for the past twenty-one years.

As Ian's passion reached fever pitch, and he became almost hysterical every time the ball got close to Barnsley's box, I found myself paying less attention to what the players were doing and increasingly drawn to a compact group of around 250 fellow Leeds fans in another part of the stands.

Unlike 99% of the other fans at the game, who were wearing dull, morose, practical clothes to keep them warm and comfortable on a cold October afternoon, these were wearing a splendidly bright array of colours. They were dressed from the neck to the toes in designer brands, from Puma G Vilas footwear to Sergio Tacchini tracksuit bottoms. Those who weren't kitted out in top-of-the-range sportswear were clad in light blue, bleached jeans and white trainers.

We were close enough for me to see that this gang weren't there for the football. They didn't appear to be interested in anything happening on the pitch, and they weren't joining in with the chanting and singing. It would be fair to say that they were doing their best to intimidate, standing solidly as one, posing in their designer gear with their eyes fixed on the home crowd. Although none of them looked particularly intimidating as individuals – they were the antithesis of the usual stereotypes associated with fighters, looking as though they'd just stepped out of a catalogue – there was a sense of menace about them. They looked hard as fuck, and I was mesmerised by them.

The first thing that went through my head was, *Who the fuck are they?* They were clearly a gang of sorts. I mean, you don't get hundreds of people all wearing the same type of gear in the same place by accident. And it wasn't as though there was a section for goths. The group that was standing a hundred yards or so from us was a unit, there was no doubt about that, and when they invaded the pitch, not once but twice, they confirmed what kind of a unit they were. These were hardcore disruptors. Football hooligans.

As the players did their best to keep away from the swarm of branded fluorescence spilling out onto the pitch mid-game, officials in equally bright but less high end hi-vis jackets, supported by several members of South Yorkshire's finest, did their best to stem the tide and bring back some order. Far from deterring the group that I would later learn was called the Very Young Team (VYT), the chase only added to the fun. Teens in Pringle jumpers and casual attire were taunting their pursuers while giving them the finger as they dribbled their way around the turf with almost as much agility as the players. But rather than trying to score goals, they were determined to reach the home end for a fistfight.

Almost like the screaming thrill-seekers who, for at least the first few seconds as their carriage creaks its way up a rickety rollercoaster rail, wish they were somewhere else, or like cinema-goers who delight in having the shit scared out of them by a horror film but spend half of the movie squinting at the screen from behind their fingers, I was almost put off by the behaviour of the VYT. Almost.

Despite the wrongness of it all, the fact that they were interrupting the flow of the game and spoiling it for everyone else, and the other similar reasons why I felt repulsed by what they were doing, I was also undeniably attracted to them. Was it their freedom of expression, strength as a team, or wildness that was appealing to me? Or was my mind simply blown by the surreal combination of style, fashion and expensive branding with anarchy?

## A new suit of armour

Even though it was forty years ago, the feeling I got when I first saw the VYT is as vivid now as it was then. I may not have understood what I was experiencing or even have been able to put it into words as a sixteen-year-old, but I recognised it for what it was: a kind of calling. My goth-punk identity had served its purpose for the previous four years or so (I still love the colour black), but as I stood in Oakwell Stadium that day, I saw a completely different look and felt a deep attraction to it. These youths had an energy – call it a *je ne sais quoi*, if that floats your boat. They had a charisma that I wanted to tap into, and becoming a part of the VYT was inevitable from the moment I set eyes on them.

While I have referred to the Leeds casuals as 'lads', that's not strictly accurate because there were female members. For example, there were a couple of young women from Bradford, who I believe were sisters. I later learned that they were notorious for infiltrating the crowds of the other teams and creating chaos at away games. Nobody expected violence from a couple of young ladies, so they didn't see them coming, and once shit kicked off, these two were extremely hard to deal with. After all, how could eighties-era men respond to being taunted and disrespected by a couple of young women? They couldn't exactly beat them up, could they? But nothing lasts forever, and women's rights had evolved by the time we faced Middlesbrough away, when we all witnessed them being punched full-on in the face by Middlesbrough's finest.

It wasn't just the aura of the VYT members that was pulling me towards them but the freshness, cleanness, and vitality of the brands they were wearing. Psychologists, sociologists, and other social scientists have all tried to figure out the link between football hooliganism and designer labels. I'm no psychologist, but I can tell you what I saw on that October afternoon.

Without wanting to be overly political, because I'm no politician either, I saw a large number of otherwise lost, disaffected, young men who, like me, were trying to figure out their place in a rapidly changing world. This was a time when industries that had thrived for generations were dying, job opportunities were scarce, and wealth was worshipped. Wearing expensive designer labels gave them a stake and bonded them into a tribe.

My way of getting through my teens had been to embrace the goth look, at least as far as my taste in music and attire were concerned. It felt right, and that's the important word here – *felt*. Not everyone is a writer, an introspective person, particularly articulate, or even self-aware. While some can pinpoint and express exactly how they feel and what they're about within a few paragraphs of perfectly constructed, richly descriptive sentences that reach into the soul and bring out the truth, others show us how they feel with a few grunts and a punch in the face.

Feelings are unmistakable, even when they are beyond words, which they often are, like the taste of someone's favourite food or the way the hairs on the back of their neck stood on end the first time they heard The Damned's 'New Rose'. While we might not be able to describe some truths, we can know them, just as surely as you can tell at a glance whether the dog that's wagging its tail so energetically is going to jump all over you and cover your face in saliva or try to bite your bollocks off at the first opportunity it gets. Feelings don't lie, and we know when we are where we belong. We know when we have found someone we want to be with. We know when we have found our tribe.

Like a lot of people who attended school, I was the victim of bullying from the moment I turned up for the first day. Adopting the goth look gave me some protection. As I passed through puberty, it also helped me to match my outward expression with my inner world of feeling, but it wasn't a perfect match. Not by any stretch of the imagination. When I saw that brightly coloured group of young men wearing expensive sports brands and posing and moving around as one, as tightly bonded as any army, that was something else entirely. I felt it in my gut, my heart and my head. This was *my* tribe. These were *my* people. I couldn't explain why or how this was true, or draft a thesis on their philosophy and attitude to life, but I knew I wanted to be like them and with them.

Black had provided me with a vehicle to express myself as an individual. Now that I had found my tribe, trendy designer gear offered me a way to connect with them. Black was replaced with bright colours, and I couldn't wait to don the same 'uniform' as the charismatic group of men I'd seen at the game.

On the bus home, Ian rabbited on about his team's conquest, only pausing to complain about 'those wankers' who had invaded the pitch. Most of it washed over me as I tried to disguise the fact that I was already daydreaming about my first VYT-inspired fashion statement.

Later that day, while Ian was probably repeating that same narrative to his parents, siblings, mates, and whoever would listen, I managed to convince my mum to bleach my jeans. By the next morning, they were sky blue. One small step for the jeans, and one giant leap for Julian Kynaston!

# TWO

# Bound By Brands

From those sink-bleached jeans that Mum had sorted for me after the Leeds game, other innovations followed. My newfound passion for upmarket brands even led to me attempting to stitch the Armani eagle onto a jumper using wool (I'm cringing as I write this). I've no idea what my parents thought of the new Julian. They probably dismissed it as typical teen behaviour, but I don't think they would have known anything about the football casual subculture.

## Fashion funds

Let's face it, the YTS scheme wages weren't enough for the kind of clothes I wanted to wear – or anything, for that matter. I was paid £17.50 per week, which would be around £42 in today's money. Even before the crazy inflation and cost-of-living crisis that the UK is experiencing at the time of writing, you couldn't buy much with that kind of cash. Other than the money I borrowed from my nan, my clothing budget was whatever I was given for Christmas and birthdays, and that was spent within a day or two of receiving it.

It doesn't cost much to be a goth, but the fashion taste of your average casual was on another level. A lambswool jumper from Pringle was typically priced somewhere between £50 and £100, and a Burberry Golfer – the seminal football jacket (my 'battle armour'), which for me symbolised the casual look more than any other garment – could set you back another £200. For context, you'd be looking at up to £350 for a similar Pringle lambswool jumper today and around £1,200 for the Golfer if the line hadn't been discontinued in the early 2000s. Being a casual was not for people with more sense than money. How the fuck was a trainee screen printer going to pull together that kind of cash?

One of the methods I used to generate income serves as an excellent illustration of how crazy the drive was to get our hands on pricy fashion brands. Somehow, I managed to obtain a Next store card. That meant I could buy their gear on credit, but I wasn't interested in their fashion lines. What I really needed was cash or, failing that, a credit card, and no bank in its right mind was going to give one of those to a seventeen-year-old with one O level in geography and a YTS job at a screen printers. Who could blame them? I couldn't even keep up the repayments to my nan.

How do you convert a store card into a credit card? By buying goods on credit and selling them for cash – except that I was so desperate to make this happen in a hurry, I was buying goods with the card and flogging them at less than half price. With a credit limit of £1,200, I could generate roughly £600 in cash, and with that cash buy a few items more befitting a fine young casual. This left me with a financial hangover, as the debt would have to be settled, which is where my other enterprise came in handy.

Despite the stench of the chemicals, the tediousness of precision sweeping, and the poor wages, my job gave me the opportunity to make some extra cash. Rumour has it, and I can't confirm whether it's true, that when the boss wasn't around, I was using the screen-printing equipment to forge Robe di Kappa T-shirts. Such a creative enterprise would mean I could produce attractive, highly fashionable, and realistic copies of the coolest brands. Then I could sell them at affordable prices to generate a healthy profit and use that money to pay for genuine designer gear. More importantly, what better way to become an established member of a casual firm than being the main source of branded clothes? If such rumours were true, working at a screen printers would surely be a dream job.

Of course, I'd have to get to know the casuals first.

## Birds of a feather – the NCL

Following the Barnsley–Leeds away game, the first match I went to was Leeds against Huddersfield at Leeds Road, but, notably, I went on my own. Ian would have been there with other friends of ours, for sure, but I steered clear of them. I had already made up my mind that I was going to join the Leeds casuals.

On the day of the match, I arrived in Huddersfield early and discreetly, hanging around the train station, desperately avoiding the attention of any Huddersfield casuals. Around eleven in the morning, the VYT spilled out from the station in impressive numbers. That's when I first noticed a few female casuals. The station was heaving, and I easily blended in with everyone else as they set off towards Leeds Road. The Huddersfield Young Casuals (the HYC), were mobbing up in every ginnel and alleyway from the square to the stadium, and numerous skirmishes broke out along the way, most intensely early in the journey outside a pub called The Crescent, the HYC's self-proclaimed headquarters.

As the VYT landed early at the stadium, and it was evident that the fair was in town across the road, in an unplanned and somewhat humorous move, everyone decided to pile in there. This was the first time that I could say I felt as though I was a part of the group. I was chatting with a few of them and certainly felt no threat from the rest. One thing that will remain etched in my memory is how quickly the fun fair emptied once we arrived, leaving us with the pick of the rides.

Minutes later, we were marching *en masse* towards the stadium, but as I made my way to the away supporters' turnstiles, I noticed that most of the others were heading for the entrance to the home stands. The sheer audacity of it was mind-blowing. I thought, *Fucking hell!*

The whistle blew, and the game started. Whatever tension had been mounting had yet to be released, but I knew that as soon as shit started, it would be total carnage. As Huddersfield fans started singing 'Where's your famous service crew?', they were completely unaware that the stars of the song were in a sixty-strong group at the bottom of their stands. The inevitable happened, and all hell broke loose. It's worth mentioning here that by this time, the Leeds Service Crew (LSC) they were referring to was no more than a concept that tied the various Leeds-affiliated football gangs together and had been succeeded by the VYT.

As far as I am aware – and I am confident that any long-term Leeds or Huddersfield fans would verify this – no firm had pulled a stunt of this magnitude before (although a couple of seasons later, Newcastle went on to do the same). It was unheard of, which isn't unsurprising when you consider that once the fighting started, the VYT found themselves outnumbered by well over a hundred to one. Confidence is one thing. This was insanity. As the violence escalated and spread around the crowd, the battlefield levelled out. Even though I was nowhere near the home stand, I ended up embroiled in a fracas with police behind the Leeds goal. What a brilliant afternoon! How that game was not cancelled, I will never know.

After the final whistle had blown, I was back to being alone again, which I wouldn't have been if I had been taking the train from Huddersfield to Leeds with the rest of the Leeds fans. Every route to Denby Dale was fraught with danger as Huddersfield fans were everywhere, and I was likely to get my head stoved in. I decided to head for my grandparents' house in Netherton instead, as that seemed a safer option.

At that time I used to spend around half the week staying with my grandparents, and I noticed that, unlike Denby Dale, where dressers were few and far between, Netherton had more than its fair share of casuals. The village had its own firm, the Netherton Casuals Limited, or NCL as they were known, who were mainly but not exclusively Leeds United supporters. As I boarded the bus, a group of NCL casuals were also getting on, and the effort I had put into trying to look like a casual didn't go unnoticed.

'Alright, mate. Who are you?'

If there was one thing that would earn respect among dressers, it was being prepared to stand your ground –

even if that meant taking a kicking. Even if these had been Huddersfield dressers, I would have told them I was Leeds. As it happened, we were on the same side. 'I'm Leeds,' I answered. They let me sit with them on the bus; one of them handed me a can of cheap lager, and several strong friendships were formed.

Shortly after that first interaction with the NCL, I became an accepted member of the firm – but not before they took the piss out of my clothes. Nothing I was wearing was right. From the colour to the material, the brand, and the type of garment, there was no escaping the onslaught of brutal ribbing. This, I discovered later, is part and parcel of the NCL's onboarding process, but it didn't end after the initiation. One of the features of casual culture was that no sooner had you reached the standard and were able to show up on point, sporting the right labels, than the goalposts would be moved. You were continually up against a moving feast.

Like the rest of the UK, most towns and villages around Huddersfield had their own firms of casuals, and apart from the NCL in Netherton, they were exclusively supporters of Huddersfield Town. The names were as original and inventive as it gets – the Golcar Mafia, the Slathwaite Suicide Squad (SSS), and the Marsden Centre Firm were three of the firms based in the Colne Valley. Huddersfield's firms collectively formed the HYC, and they hated the NCL because of its allegiance to Leeds United.

Every gang had a calling card, and I mean that literally. The NCL's glossy cards carried the words 'Netherton Casuals Limited' in a fancy, flamboyant, italicised font. I know because not only did I own some and enjoy handing them out, but I designed and printed them for everyone else.

## Loyalty to the cause

I found most of the lads in the NCL easy to get on with. They were young men, just like me, who were doing what they could to earn a living and had otherwise ordinary lives. Some were quietly spoken, introverted people while others were anything but. What bonded them, and it was a very strong bond, was their loyalty to each other and to an idea that was greater than any one member – the football team.

Whoever we were as individuals in 'civvy street' was put aside once we were 'dressed'. Most people were on a similar rung on the ladder workwise, and most jobs were related to engineering or textiles, with a few desk jobs for those who'd bothered with university or further education. Something we all had in common was our drive to get on in life and, different as we may have been in our everyday lives, we were united in our smart casual clothes. That was the investment. Keeping up with the fashion was expensive, as labels went in and out of favour quickly. It was a relentless project, underpinned by a culture of one-upmanship.

The more expensive the brand, the more indestructible we felt – and if you were wearing Giorgio Armani, you could take on anyone.

As long as you made the effort and showed your allegiance, you were fully accepted. That acceptance, that feeling of being a part of something, of supporting a cause – it could have been anything – was intensely empowering. That's why Terence could be a shy and retiring trainee accountant between nine to five, the sort of man any young lady could take home to her parents, and a fucking savage after seven in the evening. If Red Bull gives you wings, Fila and Lacoste were providing us with body armour. Most of us weren't tough guys until we were drugged on brands.

## Initiation

In 1989, Alan Clarke's gritty film about casuals, *The Firm*, was released.[2] It was more of an underground film, hardly pushed by mainstream media. It has a very fly-on-the-wall, documentary feel to it and stars Gary Oldman as the leader of a fictional firm called the 'Inter City Crew', based on West Ham's notorious ICF (Inter City Firm).

*The Firm* offers a realistic glimpse into the world of casuals, but it also influenced how firms operated. It

---

2.  A Clarke, *The Firm*, BBC (1989)

was banned in several countries because of the level of violence in some of the scenes, including one that depicted an initiation ceremony where recruits had to fight several other gang members at once and have the letters 'ICC' cut into their arms. It was a must-watch for casuals, and crews up and down the country adopted that initiation ceremony. I myself had the letters 'NCL' carved into my arm with a Stanley knife.

Another initiation involved standing in a room with the light turned off and having to throw darts at each other. It doesn't take much imagination to guess at some of the horrendous injuries that resulted from this misadventure. When the light was switched back on, everyone would be standing around like hedgehogs with darts sticking out of them, and the first thing I'd do was burst into fits of laughter. Not because having a dozen darts sticking out of me was any fun at all. That's just how I respond to adrenaline. Going through initiation strengthened our bond.

Within three months of my first encounters with the VYT at Oakwell Stadium and later Huddersfield, and with money coming in from the apprenticeship and 'other sources', I was dressed like a fully-fledged casual and no trace of my former goth self remained. Hundreds of pounds worth of the finest branded sports gear was crowned with a David Bowie 'flick head' – a long fringe covering one eye that meant that you had to flick your head frequently to see properly. In some ways it was quite feminine, but the shaved bits with a wedge at the back made it look as sinister as fuck, slightly psychopathic even.

## Casual battles

When most people think of football hooligans, they recall notorious firms such as Stoke City's Naughty Forty or the Millwall Bushwackers. Or they think of films like *Green Street*,[3] *The Firm*, or my personal favourite, *Awaydays*.[4] The focus is also often on violence, which is usually glorified. Of course, there was violence, plenty of it, but that's not really what it was about. If it had just been violence for violence's sake, we would all have been picking fights with everyday people in pubs, but that's not how it was.

Was I capable of violence? Yes. Was I aggressive? Not particularly. It was there, and increasingly so in my teens, as is the case for many young men, but people weren't giving me a wide berth or having to tip-toe around me. Although we were disruptive and it wouldn't have been advisable to stand in our way, we were only interested in fighting other casuals, and all the conflict was football-related. We also felt as though we were fighting *for* something, strange as that might sound. What mattered wasn't how many punches were thrown but that both sides were prepared to stand up

---

3. L Alexander, *Green Street*, Universal Pictures (2005)
4. P Holden, *Awaydays*, Optimum Releasing (2009)

for themselves, to fight for what they believed in, even if that thing was something as seemingly unimportant as a football team.

One of the biggest firms I ever faced was West Ham's ICF, which, incidentally, also had a significant minority of females. Leeds were playing West Ham at home, and four of us had arrived at Elland Road early, around ten in the morning, to collect tickets. We suddenly noticed a huge mob making their way towards us, and quickly realised it was the ICF. I clearly remember turning to a guy called Jock and saying, 'We're not fucking moving. We're gonna stand our ground, but I'll see you in hospital.' That's exactly what we did. Ridiculously outnumbered, we stood our ground in the face of certain annihilation. The gang picked up momentum and went from walking to marching to jogging and were soon running at us in full battle mode.

It was like one of the final scenes in the 1964 historical war film *Zulu*,[5] which stars Michael Caine as a soldier in the Battle of Rorke's Drift of 1879. In the movie, a small group of British soldiers were trying to hold their position surrounded by thousands of less well-armed but highly skilled and utterly fearless Zulu warriors. After withstanding several waves of advancing Zulus, taking casualties and some losses along the way, the British soldiers are spared. In what appears to be a nod of respect, the Zulu soldiers chant some kind of

---

5.　C Enfield, *Zulu*, Paramount Pictures (1964)

war song, turn around and walk away. It is a powerful scene.

Equally miraculously for me and my mates, as the ICF were charging towards us at full pelt, in what can only be described as a collective change of heart, they all stopped running within a few metres of us, and anger turned into laughter. We all ended up shaking hands and having a good chat. There was nothing to stop them from giving us a pasting. We had stood our ground, so whatever came our way was fair as far as casual culture was concerned. Looking back on it, the ICF were pretty sporting that day, and I got to keep my cheekbones intact for a few more years!

Most of the fighting that took place was between rival firms locally, and it didn't only happen on match days. Leeds United is a vast club, and it was even then, but there was no one firm, in my opinion, that could legitimately say they 'ran Leeds'. It was more the case that many satellite gangs had formed, which identified as either the LSC or, increasingly, VYT, and the rivalry was often fierce, even among the different Leeds-affiliated casual gangs. The fact of the matter is that we considered our group to be 'the' Leeds representatives for Huddersfield, and we were proud of it – that's all that mattered to us.

## Casual alliances

The casual scene had its own rules. You could be beating the shit out of someone one day, or taking a kicking from them, and be best mates the next. Some casuals from firms that were sworn enemies interacted in other areas of their lives. Jokes would be exchanged, social pleasantries engaged in, and genuine mutual respect shown. The story of how I became friends with the lads from Slathwaite is worth sharing on this point.

A few of us were out in Netherton one night when we came across a couple of brothers who got a bit mouthy with us. When the fighting broke out, one thing led to another and these two ended up running into a local chippy with some of us in pursuit. As things got more intense, one of my mates was on the verge of shoving this guy's head in the boiling chip fat. Fortunately, everyone came to their senses before anything horrific could happen.

The brothers were not impressed, as you can imagine, and they ran off into the night shouting stuff like 'You're all fucking dead,' and 'We'll be back.' Well, if you were a casual, you heard that kind of crap all the time, but the old motto 'All is fair in love and war' tended to apply to most situations. Unfortunately for us, in this one, it didn't – they came back with a massive entourage of the Colne Valley's finest, the Marsden Centre Firm and the SSS.

If you've ever watched any of the films about the Kray twins, you will have seen them getting tooled up and piling into convoys of shiny black luxury cars in the 1960s. Not so for these casuals. They showed up in a furniture removal van! As they jumped out of the back of the vehicle, which had screeched to a stop only metres from us, half a dozen of my mates made themselves scarce, leaving just a couple of us to face the gang alone.

This mob meant business, and there was no hope of the kind of de-escalation and handshake that we'd enjoyed at West Ham. Oh no – it's fair to say we were fucked. A few of us took a pasting that night, but we stood up for ourselves and gave back what we could for the first ten seconds or so before everything went dark and confusing.

There was only one way to earn real respect as a casual, and that was through loyalty and bravery. Sure, we had grievous bodily harm inflicted on us that night, but we also won a hell of a lot of respect, because we could have run. We could have acted like sensible people, apologising and begging them to spare us (though that would have been pointless, the shame of surrender was similar among casuals to that of Samurai culture) – but we didn't. We gritted our teeth, looked them right in the eyes, and went into battle.

Once the savagery was over, we became friends. I guess all is fair in love and war after all, but we had to take our medicine first. The Trojan Horse they used to bring their crew to Netherton belonged to the father of one of the lads in the SSS. He ran a removal business, and he used to let his son, 'Thomas the Tank Engine', use the van in the evenings.

Becoming friends with the SSS came with many benefits. First, we had one gang fewer to fight, and second, in joining forces we had greater numbers. But best of all, we had Thomas the Tank Engine's removal van, so we could easily get to any town or village we wanted to…and get out again.

We had many a good night with that van – and one particularly bad one. Almondbury will forever be a story that gets told and reflected on to this day. Instead of arriving and being met by casuals, we were confronted by most of the village's hard lads and dads who were not remotely impressed with our style. Most of them were twice our age, and they came to greet us armed to the teeth. The details of that night are not for this book, but let's just say they weren't just carrying knuckledusters or baseball bats.

The morning after, I turned on Channel 4's Ceefax, the most up-to-date and advanced text-based news service of its time, because, to my mind, certain events from the previous night should have made the national news. After a nerve-wracking two hours of staring at and refreshing the screen for updates, I calmed down, satisfied that we weren't going to get into as much trouble as we could have done.

## An unexpected escalation

One season when Huddersfield played Leeds at Elland Road, a few of us spotted the chance to become famous. We scaled the fence, avoided the Old Bill, charged across the empty pen that segregated us and started to climb over the opposite fence before we were blocked with a few well-placed punches through the bars. The HYC were affronted and decided they were going to come to Netherton to sort us out once and for all.

A police officer, Sergeant Hartley, tracked me down to deliver a stark warning: 'You'd better watch your back, son. After removing a large group of Huddersfield fans from Polly Flinders' café and loading them onto a bus home, a dozen or so flick knives were recovered from the premises.' The HYC had discarded their weapons, knowing the police were going to search them.

The aggravation between the NCL and the HYC escalated, and that night, a group of them had showed up at my grandparents' house looking for me. Fortunately, they didn't get what they wanted that night. Things were getting out of hand, and I was falling out of love with the casual subculture. Where was it all going to end? The last straw came at a Leeds home game.

## A culture change

It was 1989. After years in the doldrums of the second division, with gate numbers hitting all-time lows, Leeds United's relatively new manager, Howard Wilkinson, had managed to turn things around. The team was playing better, and this was driving an increase in ticket sales and popularity for the club. That led to an influx of glory supporters and wannabe casuals into the VYT, but with them came a change in culture.

Look, I'm not saying that we were saints or that our behaviour didn't impact the wider community – I own that, even though it was almost forty years ago – but we did stand for something. Or at least it felt as though we did. I started following Leeds during those dark years when the club was stuck in the second division with no hope of promotion. We were the underdogs.

The first time I saw the VYT at that Barnsley game in 1983, one of the things that impressed me was how brave and united they were even though they were massively outnumbered. Likewise, Netherton was surrounded by Huddersfield casuals. We embraced the old values of casual culture: loyalty, courage, and staying united. The violence was purposeful even if it achieved nothing. It was purposeful because it was an expression of that loyalty and camaraderie. Things had changed significantly, and as I looked around at Leeds, its supporters and its casuals, I didn't like what I saw.

There was no loyalty, camaraderie or courage, and that was obvious from how they were dressed. This new breed of 'casuals' didn't even look the part. In fact, I can't call them casuals. They were random gatherings of misfits looking for violence for its own sake. Yes, we engaged in violence, but we weren't thugs.

The last Leeds game I ever attended was a home game against Bradford. As I stood with a couple of mates of mine in the South Stand, a group of skinheads were making a lot of noise in front of us and acting like total cocks. They were singing crap songs, shouting all kinds of nonsense, and I couldn't identify with them at all. Was this what we had become? This wasn't who I was, and I didn't want to be anywhere near these dickheads.

I looked at my mates to see what they made of things, and I could tell we were all on the same page. This wasn't just me. Things were changing, for the worse. I tapped one of the boneheads on the shoulder.

'What the fuck do you want?' he growled, looking round at me.

'I'm Bradford Ointment,' I announced.

All hell broke loose. Violence erupted and chaos followed. It was the only possible outcome.

After that act of recklessness, I didn't feel the same about the Leeds casuals, and we moved on from each other. I went my way, and they let me go. But that left me in a quandary. What was I going to do? Join the HYC? They wanted to fucking kill me.

## Back to Barnsley

Would you believe me if I told you that the next time I went to a football match, it was to support Barnsley at the club's Oakwell Stadium? One of the things I had noticed during my years as a Leeds casual was how solid Barnsley's dressers were. 'The Five O' was well ahead of other firms. No matter where Leeds went, we would always take numbers, but on the two occasions that we'd visited Barnsley since that first encounter when I saw two VYT pitch invasions, The Five O was one of the few firms that turned out to meet us, and its members were not the least bit intimidated by being outnumbered. At the time, I used to assume that many of these guys were the sons of miners and faced no threat whatsoever going home to say they'd been in bother or even arrested. They might even have received a pat on the back and a 'well done' from their dads. Barnsley's casuals were cool, and I always leaned towards cool.

Knowing that some of the rival gangs in Huddersfield had their knives out for me – literally – and were even prepared to come to my grandparents' house to get to me had taken its toll. Having been in the game for so long, a known face among casuals and probably the police too, I felt as though I was only a couple of games away from the kind of injury that is difficult to bounce back from, or a prison sentence. It was time to put down my war paint and go back to being an ordinary football supporter.

As I said, this is not a book about football hooliganism, and so this is where that chapter of my life is being parked, but it is an important one to talk about for several reasons. It was during those five or six years that I directly experienced the power of brand for the first time. Casuals recognised each other because of the brands they were wearing, and those brands united them, empowered them, and gave them a means of expression. Even members of rival gangs could become friends because we were all Pringle boys, even if we were fighting on different sides.

To this day, I am still friends with many of my old NCL comrades, and I even became mates with the HYC along the way. I got to know The Five O, but just as friends – no violence. They knew my backstory, though, and they gave me my fair share of stick and ribbing for it too, and they still do.

You might be surprised to learn that I frequently discover that some of the most senior people I deal with – clients of mine, chief executives, founders, and managing directors – were once part of the casual subculture. Just as I did, they put their uniforms back in the wardrobes and focused their energy on more constructive enterprise, applying the fearlessness of the warrior mindset they had adopted to more important things. Things that matter. Now, they have jobs, careers, families, and more wholesome hobbies than smashing their bare fists into other people's faces. But you never forget your first youth culture and reminiscing about a time when we lived much more carelessly can still form the basis of genuine friendships.

The warrior mindset is essential for anyone who wants to make a difference. For us, casual culture became our rite of passage. For others, it could have been boxing or the local swimming team or athletics club. My passion was (and is) branding, and in the chapters that follow, I will share how I went from casual warrior to brand warrior, ready to stand up and be counted in support of the brands I care about. Standing with them on their front line, backing brands who were the underdog, and fighting for brands who were lacking courage.

# THREE
# Becoming Respectable

'Fuckin' 'ell, Kinny. Where have you been?' one of my mates shouted as I stepped into the pub. 'We thought you weren't coming...and actually, it's your round!' There were around fourteen of them, so it was going to be an expensive night. It was a Sunday, which meant having a few drinks down at a place called The Black Bull. None of us was put off by the prospect of going to work with a hangover the next day, not while we were working for other people. You'd just stay under the radar for a few hours in the morning.

The Black Bull was in Berry Brow on the border of Newsome. We didn't like Newsome, and they didn't like us, so we'd usually get into at least one altercation with their lads when we drank there. With that in mind, we always used to go mob-handed and walk in together, but I was late that night. I wasn't planning on a long stay but considering the news I wanted to share with them, getting beers in for everyone wasn't a bad move. With recent events and the change of culture within the ranks of the VYT, I'd decided to put my career before football violence and inter-village rivalry. I was planning a major life change.

## Making my exit

In fully immersing myself in the casual scene, I had severed relationships with anyone who wasn't also a part of it. It had become a way of life. Even if I hadn't cut ties myself, people would distance themselves from me once they knew what I was involved in. They couldn't understand it, and I couldn't expect them to. In the eyes of ordinary folk, we were hooligans who ruined it for everyone else. But now I wanted out.

There was no rule to say I couldn't leave. It wasn't as though I had joined an organised crime syndicate and sworn an oath of *Omertà* as they allegedly do in the Mafia, and I didn't have to worry about my manhood being cut off or any other disastrous punishments either. At the same time, it did feel as though I was leaving a family, and I didn't want to just say, 'Oh, well. That's me done. I'm gonna be respectable from now on. All the best!' even if that was a fairly accurate account of why I was leaving the firm. I needed a bigger reason.

I'd mentally rehearsed a spiel, and the right moment came for me to make my move. The piss-taking and small talk had fizzled out, and the focus was turned to the next 'outing'.

'Guys, I can't come with you next week...'

That got everyone's attention because, for the last few years, I had proved myself to be one of the most committed members of the NCL. 'I'm starting my own business, lads.' The slight pause I allowed to give the message a chance to sink in was interrupted as soon as someone very quickly sussed where I was going with this announcement.

'So, what does that mean, Kinny?

'Well, I can't be going to meetings looking like this, can I?' and I pointed to my face. The white sclera of my left eye was seriously discoloured, and the skin around the eye and cheekbone was an interesting blend of various shades of red, purple, green, and yellow. My face was also slightly swollen and misshapen, as I'd broken both of my cheekbones. Ironically, though, none of my current wounds was the result of a fight with casuals.

A few days earlier, I'd taken the girl I 'd been seeing for a night out in Holmfirth, and we ended up in a crowded basement boozer. The mistake I made – a major one – was to forget that people who didn't know anything about casual culture would have no fears or hesitations about getting into a scrap with one. Donning a brand made *me* feel indestructible, but they didn't give two fucks – to them, I was just a bloke in loud clothing. When some of these, what I would call 'farming types', started harassing my girlfriend and a couple of them pinched her arse, the fuse was lit.

'What the fuck do you think you're playing at? Come on. I'll take the lot of you outside.' The only thing that got taken outside was my head, and about ten of them played football with it for several minutes. I learned an important lesson that night: dressing, theatre, and reputation only work if others recognise what it symbolises.

Even so, the point I'd made to my mates in The Black Bull was valid. If I wanted to be taken seriously in business, I couldn't be showing up to meetings with a smashed face. There are only so many times you can tell someone you got injured playing rugby, and I know fuck all about that game, so throwing out that excuse too regularly would be a risky move indeed.

I wasn't sure how the crew would react to me wanting to pack it all in, but within seconds of me announcing my 'retirement', one of them said, 'Well, you know where we are if you have a bad debt.' Other than asking me to tell them about what I was going to be doing, that was that. My explanation was fully accepted, and they all wished me well.

With my mission accomplished and a couple of pints down my neck, all I needed to do next was start a business. It couldn't be that difficult, could it?

## Dave Ellis – a legend round the corner

As I entered my teens, long before the casuals were even on my radar, I used to hang out with a lad called Steve Ellis and would spend a lot of time at his house. Steve's older brother, Dave, was a legend in Huddersfield, having established himself as the city's first punk, even managing to wing a bit part in the opening minutes of the iconic Sex Pistols film of 1979, *The Great Rock 'n' Roll Swindle*.[6]

Dave was the first person I knew who had a record player in his bedroom, and he had an excellent collection of punk vinyl singles and albums to play on it. Whenever he left the house, Steve and I would seize the chance to enter his bedroom and listen to his music at full volume – Siouxsie and the Banshees, The Clash, and, of course, The Pistols. Dave soon cottoned on to what we were doing, and he'd usually say something along the lines of, 'Keep your grubby mitts off my records. If I find one scratch on them, there'll be trouble.' And he was as good as his word, even going as far as tying us up on one occasion. He scared the shit out of

---

6.   J Temple, *The Great Rock 'n' Roll Swindle*, Virgin Films (1980)

us at the time, but that's part of being the older brother, and we were easy targets.

It wasn't just the music that was cool about Dave's room. It was the look and feel of the place, filled with posters and other punk paraphernalia. Like I went on to be, Dave was a screen printer and did stuff for many of the local businesses. He was also a designer and had created the advertising artwork for a local band called Xpozez, who made fast, energetic, hardcore punk music. As soon as I saw the black text on the Day Glo yellow background, I was attracted to everything about it, even the smell of the screen-printing ink and the paper itself. He'd used a hand-cut font, and the attention to detail was superb. The look and feel of the artwork captured my imagination in the same way that the loud branding of casual culture would scream out to me later. It was as though I was primed to appreciate artwork, graphic design, and all things related to branding.

If you believe that preferences can be passed down genetically, the lineage was certainly there in my case. My mother's family founded the Holmfirth Art Gallery, and my maternal grandad, Henry Sykes, and his dad, Peace Sykes, were the most locally well-known artists of their generations. In an old newspaper clipping that I still have, Peace is described as the best-known landscape artist, especially in the medium of watercolour, that Huddersfield has produced:

'Notwithstanding the vagaries and changes
of style that come and go, and the different
schools with their –ists and –isms that arise,
develop and either fade away or, as the best do,
leave some permanent imprint on the history
of art, yet the works of Peace Sykes give to the
lover of pure watercolour drawings as much
pleasure today as they afforded when they left
the artist's studio.'

That article was published in the first half of the last
century. Given that my great-granddad was born in
1826, it's fair to say he succeeded in leaving a lasting
impression on the art world. The article goes on to
say that his first attempts at art were made with pipe
stems on the stone floor of his home when he was a
child. Peace always said that his success as an artist
was partly thanks to the help and encouragement he
received from his older sister, who enrolled him as a
student at the Huddersfield Mechanics Institution. She
was not well off but gave him money to buy the pencils,
paper, and colours he needed for his studies.

According to the newspaper clipping, Peace was working full-time but studied in the evenings under 'G D
Tomlinson, for whom he had the greatest admiration.'
He used to walk to Huddersfield from Netherton several
times a week to get to classes – a round trip of five miles.

I used to love it when Grandad, who worked in a fac-
tory making machinery for scoring and cutting paper,

would bring home massive piles of different-sized sheets. These blank canvasses would soon be covered with whatever artistic ramblings I needed to express. By the time I was in my mid-teens, and thanks in no small part to the influence of Dave Ellis, I was very into art, and Grandad and Nanna bought me a set of Staedtler graphic design pens for my sixteenth birthday. Even just one of those pens could cost £10 or more, and my grandparents weren't loaded, so it is humbling to think how much of a stretch it must have been to get me a full set.

As far as YTS schemes go, I was more fortunate than most in that at least I was working in an industry that interested me. After graduating from my apprenticeship, I started working for a more professional screen printer called Autosigns, as a fully trained staff member. Whenever a piece of artwork had been designed for an agency, I would claim the job before anyone else could even think about reaching for their car keys. My boss must have wondered what was so special about the ad agencies, but the truth is that their offices were as cool as fuck.

The first time I entered a design agency, it blew my mind, and I knew I wanted to work in one of these modern creative palaces. Everything about the layout and the choice of décor was designed to encourage free thinking, imagination, and creativity. Even the people working there looked stunning, dressed to the nines in the latest fashions. These offices had a pulse, and I felt it.

## Seeds taking root

My artistic family lineage, a passion for drawing, a desire to express myself – first as a goth and punk, and later as a dresser – the huge influence of Dave Ellis, and my encounters with advertising and brand agencies, were like seeds that were planted in my young mind. At some point during my casual years, those seeds germinated, and when I decided to start my own business as a twenty-two-year-old man, I knew exactly what I wanted to do.

If I had to pinpoint a key moment, I'd say it was when I first handled the Xpozez artwork in Dave's room. Just as I had known with all my heart that I wanted to be a casual and was determined to figure out a way to become a part of that scene, I felt the same attraction and determination to succeed in the world of brand and design. I was about to launch an agency, and I even had a name for it.

'Propaganda' may sound like a clever name for a branding agency, and I think it is, but don't be under any illusion that it was the product of deep thinking and a flash of inspiration. It was given to me on a plate by the German band of the same name who had some commercial success in the UK in the 1980s with tracks such as 'Duel' and 'Dr Mabuse'. Far from imagining that I was some kind of creative genius, people should be asking why the fuck no one else had snapped it up as an agency name before.

Almost every penny I'd earned at Autosigns had been spent on expensive clothing, so I didn't have any savings to draw on to fund my big idea. But my boss was supportive and gave me some money, around a grand, to help me along. Even accounting for the crazy inflation we've experienced recently, a grand would still be worth less than £2,000 in today's money, so I was working on a super-tight budget.

## Build it and they will come

A local mill owner took a chance on me and gave me three months' credit on the rent for a large open-plan area in a disused mill in Meltham, so I had an office space. It was an empty shell, but it had character. Anyway, if I didn't have the spark to own it and make it look special, what was the point in setting up a creative agency? I took every penny I had and ploughed it into crafting the perfect office space for Propaganda. It was very much a 'build it and they will come' approach, rooted in faith and determination. Once the office was suitably 'dressed', it would become invincible, and success would surely follow.

The first few weeks passed, and 'they' didn't come. What had I expected? There were plenty of agencies, business relationships had already been established, and my prospects were either using someone else or trying to do stuff in-house. We were a brand-new agency, so we had a mountain to climb. 'Who have you worked for?', 'What have you done?' and 'Can anyone recommend you?' were typical and reasonable questions.

Those weeks turned into months, and as I approached the end of the first quarter, it looked like we were going to hit a wall. They say Rome wasn't built in a day, but as we approached the end of the third month, I hadn't even built a house, let alone a village, town or city. The rent was about to become due, the landlord would be expecting at least something to pay back his investment, and I couldn't even show him an order.

With days to spare, the breakthrough that I so desperately needed came along in the form of a design-and-print project worth £17,000. That was more than I had earned in a year in my print-screening job, and I was high on the idea that I'd be earning the pro-rata equivalent of a £100,000 salary…a pleasant but misguided thought.

I had two months to deliver on my side of the deal. There would be overheads, mainly printing costs, and I was going to need staff, but I wouldn't have any money until I was paid once the job was finished. I was going to have to beg, borrow, and steal to make it happen. I hired a temporary member of staff to do the design work, and a couple of others joined me in the office.

No one was going to get paid for two months, so everyone else was as invested and committed as I was. We had a lot of hard work ahead of us, but the prize was worth it – seventeen grand, and the prospect of further work.

I was in business.

# FOUR
# A New Kind Of Warfare

'I'm sorry. I ain't got time to do it.' The voice in my head screamed, *Are you fucking kidding me? You've left it until the day before the order's due to tell me this.*

I felt sick. It had taken three months and every penny I had to win Propaganda's first order, a £17,000 contract to design and print pattern cards for Camborne Contract Furnishings. They'd given us three weeks to turn the job around, and we'd gone with the printer who had offered us the lowest price.

As the deadline crept closer, this printer had been increasingly conspicuous by his absence. After a week of unanswered phone calls and having left numerous voicemails, I turned up at his premises to confront him. When he dropped the bombshell that he hadn't even started the job, a part of me wanted to take a swing at him, but I had moved on from being that person. The new me would have to find another, more civilised solution. We had a contract to fulfil, and I wasn't going to let this clown stop me.

It was a Friday afternoon, and my contact at Camborne was expecting the order to be delivered on Monday. When the printer told me he couldn't do it, I walked away in disgust and set my heart on finding someone who could.

Within thirty minutes, I was sitting in another printer's office, walking them through the brief. They could turn it around, but it was going to cost me twice as much as I had originally been quoted, and I wasn't going to make a penny in profit. I later found out that the other printer had a close relationship with a local design agency. He'd deliberately undercharged us for the job with no intention of ever doing it.

Someone, it may have been Benjamin Franklin, once said, 'You pay to learn.' There is no truer saying in business that is worth paying heed to. I learned a harsh lesson that day, one that almost cost Propaganda its first big opportunity. The weapons were different, but the world of business was just as brutal as the casual wars on the football terraces.

It didn't take long for me to realise that I was already well-trained and primed for this new kind of warfare.

Though the sword had been replaced with the pen, the principles were the same, and I knew those principles inside-out, both intuitively and through experience.

## Into the lion's den

Early in Propaganda's history, we got a chance to speak to IBM. In the days leading up to the meeting, I learned that the company had a reputation for being an agency graveyard. Undeterred, I prepared as useful, informative, and inspiring a presentation as I could. As I made my way to their office, I cannot say there was no fear, but my main emotion was excitement.

I was charged with adrenaline because I was hardwired from my time as a casual to associate fear with thrill. The nearest that most everyday people get to real fear is a close scrape on the motorway, the thought of being fired, or someone looking at them the wrong way in the pub. My idea of fear, my benchmark, my frame of reference for all matters frightening, was facing a couple of hundred members of West Ham's ICF. That's danger – not a bunch of suits in a posh office. Of course, I wanted to win the contract. I wouldn't have wasted my time travelling several hundred miles to see them if I was not serious about working with them. But I was excited to succeed, not scared to fail.

After parking the car, I got my stuff together, took a deep breath, committed to the goal, and confidently strode up to the main entrance. I was warmly welcomed by the receptionist, and when my primary contact arrived to greet me, he was friendly and engaging. As he glided towards the seating area, we both smiled at each other, and I got up to meet him.

He gave his name for clarity, but I knew who he was. 'Pleased to meet you,' he declared as we shook hands. 'We're all excited to hear what you've got to offer, Julian.' *Not a bad start at all*, I thought, as he led me to a pristine boardroom where several of his colleagues were sitting around a conference table with pads and pens and glasses of water. That's when the fun started.

As I was introduced to each member of the team, I became aware of one pair of eyes burning into me in a hostile manner, as though they resented my presence in the room. When their turn came to be introduced to me, they scowled and presented a wet fish of a handshake without a word. That was the first of many openly rude attempts to show their disinterest in me, the meeting and anything I had to offer. At every opportunity, they were blatantly determined to sabotage my presentation by sneering and chucking out sarcastic, dismissive comments while I focused on delivering with as much clarity and confidence as I could muster.

Eventually, I experienced a 'Fuck it' moment. Perhaps if he had been slightly less obnoxious, I could have let it go, but the effect of his toxicity was strong enough for me to believe I had nothing to lose, and I no longer cared either way. I stopped mid-sentence and looked him in the eye for what was only a second or two but probably felt like much longer. You could almost feel the room holding its breath.

'Do you have a fucking problem with me, or what? If you do, let's go outside and sort it out,' I said.

Deadly silence.

I was not kidding or bluffing. Society teaches us to hide our true nature, cover our bodies, hide our waste products, and pretend to be civilised in polite company. But we are mammals at heart, and apex predators at that – the so-called pinnacle of evolution. One look into my eyes told my antagonist that I was not fucking around. Our instincts tell us what we need to know, and he knew it was better to shut up, back down, and take care of his manners.

The final twenty minutes of that meeting were dour. These guys expected people to doff caps in their presence, but my time with the NCL had taught me that 'we' bow to nobody. I finished my presentation, but I am not sure anyone heard another word as they were still processing the fact that a prospective supplier had just challenged their colleague to a fight. I couldn't care less. If anything, I was more comfortable closing the meeting than I had been opening it. It had felt like a loss already, and at least this way, I had been honest and true to myself.

I finished up, thanked everyone and began to put my things away, fully resigned to this being the last time I would see or speak to anyone in that office.

'Julian, can I have a word, please?' It was my main contact, and he gestured towards the door. 'Leave that. You can pack it up later. Come with me.' I was intrigued. Was he going to have a go at me for speaking my mind? Had I shown him up? Was he going to apologise for his colleague's behaviour but say, 'Thanks but no thanks'? I had no idea, but I was curious enough to follow him to his office.

He held the door open for me and told me to sit as he made his way eagerly to his comfy leather chair.

'I'm giving you the contract.'

*Fuck me!* I didn't see that coming. Was he kidding?

'I liked what you had to say, Julian, but the clincher for me was how you dealt with Daniel. Anyone who can stand up to him the way you did gets the thumbs up as far as I'm concerned, and I believe I can speak for the rest of the team when I say that. We need someone with your courage and conviction to steer our brand. I have witnessed many excellent presentations in that room, and every agency that comes to see us talks a good talk. We want someone who can walk the walk: someone like you, Julian. Let's talk numbers and deadlines.'

With that, we sat and finetuned the arrangement.

Like opponents entering the ring to face Mike Tyson when he was the most formidable fighter on the planet, most people who had been to see IBM had already lost the deal before they set foot in the building, beaten by fear. But for me, it was a moment of insight – another Miyagi moment. I realised that in the same way that Daniel San had actually been learning karate while painting the fence and waxing the car, I'd been learning about the cut and thrust of business while being a casual. Sometimes, the best form of defence is attack, and this strategy had just secured me a contract worth several thousand pounds a month.

## Taking clients into battle

The battle armour had switched from casual gear to suits, and the new battleground was in the corporate world of meeting rooms and conference halls. But I was also fighting for something else. It was no longer a matter of loyalty to the other members of a casual firm or the football club it was aligned with. My loyalty was to my clients, and they became my team. My clients needed an extremely strong, confident, and fearless advocate with a warrior mindset to stand shoulder-to-shoulder with them in the arena of brand warfare, and I could not afford to show any weakness while fighting for their brands.

When I first encountered the casuals, I didn't understand why I felt so compelled to join them, and I didn't need to for that pull to be irresistible. The attraction was a force without words. From the moment I set eyes on them, they were all I could think about. Do you remember how you felt the day before you got your first car? Or your earliest recollection of lying awake the night before your birthday, wondering if you were going to get the gift you had set your heart on. That's how I felt about becoming a casual. I was obsessed.

When I stood up for myself with confidence and conviction in IBM's boardroom, the managing director didn't need to understand why he felt the way he did. It didn't matter. The presentation didn't matter. As he said, he'd seen plenty of superb presentations, but none of those who came before me had left with a branding contract. It was something else that pulled at him that day. It was something beyond words, a non-verbal communication that spoke squarely to his heart and mind. Just as I knew I wanted to be a casual, he knew Propaganda was the agency for IBM.

This was effectively branding in action. Branding is about creating a feeling that compels people to act. If the purpose of a watch is simply to tell the time, why do people pay thousands of pounds to own a Rolex? Does the buying decision really boil down to what the device can do or even how beautiful it looks? When someone buys a Rolex, they are acquiring much more than a timepiece or a work of art. For some, it will be a status symbol, a loud and proud announcement of how successful and wealthy they are, while others will see it as a luxury that they have earned or that they are expected to have. Every Rolex owner will have a unique reason for making the purchase, but many of them won't understand or be aware of their real motivation. People are not as logical or self-aware as they think they are.

## Logic doesn't rule

Throughout history, sages, soothsayers, psychics and other mystics have claimed to be able to help people see the future. Even in today's cynical world of technology, there are plenty of people who believe in astrology or that the local tarot reader can offer valuable insight. Among those who will queue up for a private sitting with a wise mystic are chief executive officers, presidents, and people with degrees in the sciences. You can tell them they are wasting their time and money until the cows come home. They will still swear blind that the prophecies that their guides have made have come true. It's as though they don't see the parts that are irrelevant or ridiculous, only that one part of a prediction came true, and that validates everything else and helps them make sense of an otherwise random universe.

Think about the last time you had to make a key decision. Perhaps it was a new job, a house move, or even something as trivial as accepting that offer of a dinner date. We all like to think that we are logical and make our choices based on rational deduction, but most of the time, that's bullshit. It's as though, for every crossroads we face, a multitude of emotional responses spontaneously arise within us – like different voices in our heads – and what starts as a feeling of uncertainty slowly morphs into a conviction. Once that happens, action will surely follow. We feel compelled to say yes, move in, take the job or buy the fancy shoes. Sure, logic can be the voice of reason that tells us 'That person's not reliable, they're not partner material,' or 'That new job is not going to pay enough,' or 'That beautiful house is too expensive,' but we rarely listen to it.

Do you think that if I had listened to logic as a teenager, I would have joined a gang of lads who were risking arrest and serious injury and spoiling a football game? It was crazy. I knew that, but I wanted to do it anyway. The greatest storytellers on earth, from Shakespeare to JK Rowling, understand this one fact: human beings are not logical. Even the most rational folk will often go with their hearts rather than their heads when it comes to the most important decisions of their lives.

The way I see it, my job as a brand warrior is to identify who the brand's tribe are, find them or attract them, and make them feel as strongly about the brand as I did about the casuals. It's not about logic. It's about feeling. I have to create the spark, ignite the flame, and grow it into an inferno until they feel a passion for the brand.

Brands are no different than people. If you want people to love your brand, they have to feel a connection to it, just as they would a person. If you want to understand branding, you can forget all the industry speak and smart phrases. They're just smoke-and-mirror tactics thrown up by agency folk to make you think they know a secret and help them feel special. At its core, the principle of branding is not complicated.

You can generate passion through words, images, and videos. It's about creating a feeling, an energy that is almost beyond words and something that leads to a compulsion to take action. Something touches a person on a deep, emotional level, and they immediately identify with that brand. The founder of arguably one of the first formal ad agencies, J Walter Thompson, bought a page in the *London Gazette* and split it into six segments, which he sold to other businesses at a profit. His slogan was, 'The truth well told.' As a brand agency, we want to help our clients shine in a way that expresses their truth on an emotional level. It is honest, but more than that, it touches its audience enough to make them fall in love with what they are saying and selling.

I'll be explaining more about how we did just that for ghd, Clipper, and others in later chapters. For now, I'm going to end this chapter by paraphrasing the reported words of the famous Walter Landor, the founder of Landor Associates, one of the world's leading brand consulting and design firms: products are made in factories; brands are created in the hearts and minds of consumers.

# FIVE

# Gaining Gravitas – Conquering The Boardroom

'You are sitting on a goldmine, and we've got the strategy for you to capitalise on it for many years to come. This is the perfect solution to the challenges you're facing,' I concluded, toeing a narrow line between confidence and arrogance, something which I have tried to perfect throughout my career.

I was in the antiquated boardroom of a company that had been manufacturing high-quality suited cloth for the likes of Savile Row for generations. Maybe in the past, they had made suits themselves. We never got to find out. Like many others in the textile industry, three decades ago they were facing an uncertain future because of the rapidly growing threat emerging from the Four Asian Tiger nations of Hong Kong, Taiwan, South Korea, and Singapore. However, unlike most other companies, this business had an ace up its sleeve, which we had identified.

It was sitting on hundreds, perhaps thousands of patterns for garments going back at least two hundred years, and some theatre companies, television producers, and filmmakers were using them to create authentic costumes for period dramas. No one else could tap into this market because no one else had had the foresight to archive their patterns, so they had no competition. If the costume department of a West End theatre company wanted to produce a three-piece suit from 1826 for a period drama, this manufacturer had the pattern. They could name their price, and it would be paid without a quibble. But what we discovered was that those clients couldn't care less about the heritage product that the manufacturer prided itself on creating – its carefully crafted fabrics – they were only interested in the authenticity of the patterns. It's like how people don't really care about the insurance product they're buying, they only care about the item they're protecting.

Whereas in their traditional market, they had tons of competitors, and the market was under threat, they hadn't even scratched the surface of the costume market. It was no exaggeration to say that they were sitting on a goldmine. They were dealing with tens of these filmmakers and television producers, but the truth is there were hundreds if not thousands around the globe – television, film, theatre, opera, the list goes on – and that market was theirs, all of it. But it would take a significant shift in mindset for them to capitalise on the opportunity and to turn their attention away from the product they were so proud of producing.

The alternative was to stick to what they had always known and get smashed on price and service by companies in Asia that were using state-of-the-art equipment linked to cutting-edge digital design software to manufacture high-quality fabrics and clothing at the touch of a button. They simply couldn't compete, and the random work they were getting from the entertainment industry was not going to save them without a strategy.

We knew how to realise that potential. I had offered them not just a way out but the opportunity to pivot, evolve, and thrive in an exciting future. It was a done deal as far as I was concerned, and I had no doubt that they were going to embrace the idea. All I needed was verbal confirmation. I sat there comfortably, in the middle of a pregnant pause, waiting for the boss to crack a smile and tell me how delighted he was with our proposal.

Well, I got the smile. Then, he said, 'Absolutely brilliant,' and the faces around the room all lit up. If it had been a theatre play, it would be as though he was leading a standing ovation for my performance. As the applause and the cheers of 'well done' and 'excellent' simmered down, all eyes turned back to the guy making the decisions. In an instant, the smile on his face was wiped away, replaced with a look of disinterest.

'The problem is that's not what we do. We won't be doing it, lad.'

The words hit my ears loudly and clearly, but they didn't compute. A point-blank rejection had been unthinkable. Was I hearing things?

'That's not what we do,' he repeated, and this time the message hit home. The message, sadly, was that he was too tunnel-visioned to even consider changing course from what his company had been doing for generations. Saying yes to our proposals was as unthinkable for him as his refusal was for me.

## You can lead a horse to water...

This experience proved to be typical of many of the conversations I had with the directors working in the textile industry at that time. Propaganda didn't grow from one £17k design-and-print job in Huddersfield to taking Leeds by storm overnight. We had a lot of evolving to do before that could happen, and the furnace that fired that process was the rapid demise of Huddersfield's textile industry.

Within a year of winning our first contract, we had grown to seventeen clients. Every one of them was working either directly in the textile industry – manufacturing carpet yarn or suit fabrics, for example – or they were downstream, serving the same industry by supplying things like machinery. This was unsurprising, considering Huddersfield was often referred to as the 'Mecca' of the textile industry. And it meant that our business was under just as much threat from the Four Asian Tigers as the companies we served, because they were our lifeblood.

I was first alerted to what was happening when I ventured out to see a 'dye cake' manufacturer in Leeds. Dye cake is a solid, concentrated form of dye that is still used for colouring fabrics and yarns today. The director of the company showed me a graph, which told a story of continuous growth from the birth of his business. At least, that had been the story until six months before our meeting, when the steadily rising line suddenly dropped off an invisible cliff and hit rock bottom – such was the impact of the rise of textile manufacturing in the Tiger Nations.

The director of the dye cake manufacturers could see the problem, I could see the problem, and so could the suit length manufacturer who'd dismissed my proposals. Everyone could see the problem, so why were so many companies unwilling to adapt to survive?

In my mind, the main obstacle was the breathtaking arrogance and ignorance of the industry's business leaders. The guy who had flatly rejected my suggestion that they should focus on a lucrative niche market that they had already unwittingly begun to trade in, where the buyers had actually gone to the trouble of finding them as opposed to the other way round, showed woeful delusion when he spoke about his company:

> 'Our products are made on looms that are so old, on floors that are so rickety, operated by fifth generation weavers that can almost make these machines sing, that there is no way anyone on the other side of the world can get into this game and do what we do.'

That's not a word-for-word quote, but it captures the stupidity of their perspective. How could any of that be something to boast about? In other words, he was saying that they had been so myopic and oblivious to technological change that they were still using equipment that only worked if you knew where and when to kick it into action when it stalled. They could flower it up however they wanted and try to conjure up a romantic image of their machines as being like fine wines that had matured with age. The truth was those machines were just old. While they were busy celebrating themselves for their quaint imperfections, the ones being used by the Tiger Nations were computerised with ISDN links, mounted on newly skimmed perfectly flat concrete floors, and capable of producing large volumes of identical products with astonishing efficiency. These foreign companies could make money even when selling at half the price of their British competitors. Furthermore, they could train staff to use the new machines within a week, rather than having to pass knowledge down through generations.

This guy's attitude was the norm, not the exception, and within eighteen months of that conversation, all but three of the companies we had been serving had gone out of business. As I watched it happening, unable to stop it despite my best attempts to come up with innovative solutions, I felt increasingly angry. Not so much because our customer base was disintegrating, although it was frustrating to see so many businesses – and clients – failing unnecessarily, but because of the impact these closures were having on the communities in the towns and villages that I loved. Needless job losses. A needless economic catastrophe. And who was to blame?

Initially, I believed it was all on them. Even the companies that showed a willingness to embrace change and adapt refused to acknowledge the important role a marketing strategy needed to play in their plans. A great example of this was a technical fabric manufacturer that used to supply a very thick Gore-Tex-type material. They'd invested millions into a machine that could produce the fabric at double-width. This not only provided an economic benefit in terms of how cheaply they could produce a larger volume of material, but it also had safety implications for the manufacturers they sold it to. These key benefits gave them a definitive commercial edge.

'That looks like a sound and exciting investment,' I said to the suit I'd met with, speaking from the heart, 'and the advantages are clear. So, how much are you giving us to share your news with the world?'

His response stunned me to the core. 'Fifteen grand,' he replied without so much as a smirk. I was waiting for the punchline because I thought he was joking. When neither of those things followed, I prodded: 'Are you serious? Fifteen thousand pounds?'

'Yes,' he nodded, seemingly unaware of the absurdity of what he had said. Here was a company that had had the foresight and courage to invest *millions* of pounds into an idea that would make them stronger, more profitable, and better placed for the future, but was unwilling to spend more than one thousandth of that amount on ensuring the news of their investment reached their market. To put it into perspective, back then, the cost of a full-page advertisement in the *Financial Times* was somewhere in the region of twenty-five to thirty thousand pounds. We were expected to build a powerful and effective campaign with top-tier copywriters and designers producing memorable content over a sustained period to ensure the message reached the people it needed to reach...with fifteen grand. That wouldn't even cover the preparation of the campaign, let alone rolling it out. It was madness, but the industry's leaders were too naïve to see it. They didn't understand marketing. Until then, they hadn't needed to.

We declined that brief. To have accepted it would have amounted to daylight robbery. It would have been a waste of their money and done no good for our reputation. After budgeting such a pitiful amount for the marketing of their new machine, they never even got to operate it – because they were forced into liquidation. Some clown did take that brief on. Some clown took that fifteen grand, probably knowing full well it was going to do absolutely nothing. And not a single metre of fabric went down that machine at its new width. It was the laughing stock of the industry, and our decision to stay well clear of the fallout from that debacle proved to be a wise one.

Spending on physical items such as machinery and materials was a worthwhile investment with tangible benefits, and this company understood that world. They resented spending money on marketing because they didn't understand it and couldn't relate to the benefits. They couldn't appreciate the power of branding, and that was proving to be a major stumbling block for them. They'd been catapulted into a battle they had not asked for, one that they had no chance of winning at the machine level. This battle had to be fought at an emotional level, in the hearts and minds of the consumers, but they were not prepared to invest in the weapons they needed because they didn't understand what kind of fight they were in. A fight that could only be won through effective and powerful branding.

By the nineties, it is fair to say that many of the companies in the textile industry were family businesses being run by people whose fathers, grandfathers, or even great-grandfathers had founded them. These people didn't have a passion for the industry but felt duty-bound to keep things going. Following stints at university and gap years living it up, they would be called upon to do their bit and manage the business for the next generation to inherit. As long as they could keep their companies ticking over, they preferred to spend as much time as possible on the ski slopes or sunning themselves on the French Riviera.

They weren't hungry for success, and they certainly wouldn't go hungry if their mill collapsed – they were too well-off to really be affected. Some of them didn't care at all. They'd be glad to see the back of the industry and relish the freedom to do something else instead. No, the people who suffered when those businesses failed were the workers who found themselves unemployed without a secondary trade to fall back on and nowhere to go for a job. (I've often reflected on this period of my career and wondered if it was where my left-wing leanings stemmed from.)

## A partner in battle

So, who was going to fight for the UK's textile industry? Someone had to, and whoever took on that challenge would have to embrace the power of branding. Most of the directors I had spoken to weren't prepared to do that, and I was angry with them for it, but I also realised that I was upset with myself. I had failed to make them believe in themselves and take on that fight. If I had managed to persuade them to adopt the strategies that I was recommending, I know that some of them would have survived, even if not all of them. That manufacturer with the centuries-old back catalogue of pattern templates would have thrived, for sure.

How had I failed so spectacularly? What could I have done differently? The relationships were strong, the ideas were innovative and well-thought out, and the strategies were sound. Where was the weak link? I concluded that it was a lack of gravitas, both on my part and the part of Propaganda. We were sitting in a box, suffocated by a set of expectations about what we were capable of, what we understood, and where we fitted into these companies' overall business plans.

They respected our ability to create impactful content, and they acknowledged our authority in that field, but we wanted to be seen – *had* to be seen – as more than a team of copywriters and designers. We needed to be part of the board, not just hired help for when they decided they wanted to create some pretty pictures and clever words for a press release or advertising campaign. Our clients were missing out on our greatest talents – vision and strategy. Why weren't they interested in our ideas? If we weren't positioning ourselves appropriately for them to recognise that they needed to listen to us, that was our fault.

We had to become an organisation that our clients could trust at board level, an agency that was known for being fluent in balance sheets, financial conversations, and modelling. They needed to put us at the head of the table when it came to their business growth strategies. We'd been getting hired as an add-on when we should have been at the heart of the ideation and decision-making process. If I had embodied that gravitas when I presented my proposals to boards as the textile industry was imploding around us, they would have snatched those ideas from us in a heartbeat. They'd heard the words come out of my mouth, but they hadn't listened – because it wasn't our place to talk about how they should be marketing or to whom. 'That's not what we do, lad,' said it all: 'Stay in your own lane and leave the rest to us.'

When I reflect on that period in Propaganda's history, I recognise that it's where our DNA was born. Courage is at the heart of that DNA, along with a hunger for victory. We have to inspire, motivate, and empower our clients to have the courage to take leaps of faith. If you're not in a fight, you're not pushing hard enough. Whether you're pushing or not, you can be sure that others are – they're pushing to win your clients, grab your market share, and take the lead. New threats will always show up, often when you least expect them, so you cannot afford to be complacent. That was one of the textile industry's gravest mistakes – complacency fuelled by arrogance and ignorance. When you can't outspend, you must outthink. But the industry's leaders weren't prepared to do that for themselves, or to listen to us when we tried to do it for them.

The word 'decimation' comes from the Ancient Roman practice of executing every tenth soldier as an extreme form of punishment for mutiny. The textile industry was punished far more severely than this for its failure to adapt. By the time it showed any signs of stabilising, barely 10% of businesses were still running. The ones that survived were the ones that fought hard with everything they had. These were the companies that were willing to adopt a brand-first approach, and some of these businesses were startups that rose from the ashes after the existing industry was burned to the ground.

Push your ideas to extreme levels. Be prepared to fight internally, driven by the hunger to evolve your thinking to bring out the best in your team, and be prepared to fight hard externally to win your clients over and get them on board with the boldest ideas.

I knew that the fight had to start with me. If the best perception of Propaganda I could get was that we could design cool images and put words and phrases together in a persuasive way, I may as well 'pack it in and get a proper job'. But I'm a fighter – always have been, always will be – and I wasn't ready to quit, so I set out to learn from the best in the business. The biggest brands in the world work with the biggest agencies in the world. They hire the likes of Abbot Mead Vickers (AMV BBDO), and they pay a small fortune for their services.

If I was serious about building gravitas, I had to learn from the agencies that had it in abundance, so I looked to London for the answers.

## Knowledge before assumption

I didn't have to travel down to the 'The Big Smoke' to learn how differently they were operating. After meeting someone who had worked for several leading London agencies, I learned through him about an approach to branding that tied in completely with the direction I wanted to move in, and which turned all the ideas I had seen up north on their heads. That approach was 'planning'.

'Planning' sounds like common sense when you consider how the word is usually used. Of course, campaigns are planned. Everyone understands the power of planning, don't they? Except for one thing: the kind of planning that brand agencies outside of London had been doing was missing a vital ingredient. They'd been building plans on dodgy foundations. Planning, in the sense that London agencies were applying it, is about building solid foundations first. Nowadays, we would call those foundations a 'strategy'.

The resistance I had encountered from the textile industry was down to two main issues. First, they weren't receptive to our strategic solution to their challenge, seeing us as no more than a design-and-print agency. Second, their business plans were built on assumptions and beliefs that may have been correct at one time but were becoming redundant as their markets evolved. These assumptions were the shaky foundations I am talking about.

Solving the second issue was the key to solving the first. If I had been able to convince those textile companies that their assumptions were wrong and provide robust evidence – in the form of data, in-depth research, and solid strategic argument – to support an alternative vision, they wouldn't just listen to our branding and marketing plans, they'd be hungry for them.

At the heart of planning is the principle of knowledge before assumption, and that is true whether those assumptions come from the client or the agency. As brutal as it sounds, 'That's not what we do, lad,' was a fair comment. All we were doing was replacing their assumptions with our own and building from there – even if my assumptions happened to be right. What I needed was rock-solid knowledge based on evidence. Otherwise, my clients had every right to say, 'You're not in our business, so you stick to what you do, and we'll stick to what we do.' Evidenced knowledge is what gives you gravitas, not assumptions.

London agencies had departments dedicated to planning. Before they'd even put forward a proposal, they would carry out in-depth research into the markets their prospects were operating in. They wanted to know who their prospect's customers were, what was driving them to buy their products, how they felt about the brand, what they liked, what they didn't like, and what improvements they would like to see. This much more strategic approach can be compared to the meticulous planning of a military operation.

Strategy has its roots in warfare, and the term itself comes from the Greek word *strategos*, which referred to the art of the general or military leader. Now, in the military context, it refers to the act of devising a general plan that informs several different tactical actions that all play a specific role in the pursuit of defeating an enemy or recuperating from a position of deficit. Good strategy requires an accurate assessment of the field of play to identify the challenges, inspect the enemy's strengths and weaknesses, and appraise one's own abilities to act. Planning agencies in the south were engaging in nothing short of brand warfare. They were devising strategies to help coordinate their clients' businesses around coherent plans that put their best assets and skills to work to crush the field with maximum efficiency and impact.

Agencies in the north had been approaching things the wrong way round. They'd been asking the right questions, but of the wrong people. They'd been asking their prospects and clients these questions, and the answers they'd been receiving were based on assumptions rather than facts. Some of the decision-makers we were dealing with weren't even acting on assumptions. They were asking family members from outside the business – wives, uncles, aunts, brothers, and sisters. 'Barbara, what do you think? Should we go with this shade of blue or this bright pink?'

The traditional way that branding had been done meant that the client owned the brand messaging. They could do what they wanted with it, even if that meant alienating their customer base. But if they wanted their branding to succeed, they had to recognise that their marketplace – their consumers and potential consumers – had a vested interest, and they had to consider their feelings and expectations. Our job was to help them understand those feelings and expectations and to generate ideas that would take advantage of that knowledge, sometimes by pulling in winning strategies from other industries.

## Embracing planning – acting with conviction

When Steve explained the mechanics of planning, it resonated. I realised that I had always understood this intuitively, but I didn't know it was a discipline that agencies were building departments around, or that planners were making over £100,000 a year. I knew that if we wanted to provide our clients with the best advice and persuade them to act upon it, we had to go down this route. It was one of those things that, once known and understood, couldn't be ignored. To continue as we had been, producing plans based on what we thought was the way forward rather than on evidence-based knowledge would have been fraudulent. That's how I saw it. Getting it wrong because you don't know better is one thing. Ignoring what you know because it's the easier route is something else.

I took the lesson to heart and made some radical changes. At the start of that journey, we had twenty-seven staff and forty clients. To afford the planner and a team to support them, I had to let most of our staff go. We ended up with a team of seven, which included only three of the original team, and the wage bill was identical. But it wasn't just our team that had to be transformed.

I wasn't prepared to invest that much into a high-calibre team only to work with clients that wouldn't benefit from the planning approach, or who weren't prepared to take us on as board-level partners. These numbers are no exaggeration: twenty-seven staff to seven, and forty clients to four. This wasn't just about conviction and belief in what we wanted to do, but it called upon a talent from my past – good old-fashioned bottle. We politely referred the clients we didn't want to work with any longer to other agencies that we felt were better placed to provide them with the service they wanted. This new direction was fraught with risk, but we were repositioning ourselves to serve the clients who appreciated what we could do and were prepared to act on our advice.

Part of that shedding process was recognising who we were as an agency and honouring our values. Sticking up for the underdog and standing up for what I believe in was already hugely important to me in my personal life; now it was time to embrace that professionally as well.

When a client of ours told me that they were into fox hunting, I didn't hesitate to tell them bluntly where they could stick their business, and they had to find another agency. Being open and honest about who I am is just as important to me as helping clients to identify the essence of their brand. The same characteristics that make your customers and clients love your brand and feel compelled to buy your products and services will also be the reason why others can't stand you. You can't have the love without the hate. If your brand can't embrace that, it's not strong enough. You must be clear and honest about who you are. I call it the 'shit filter'. I don't go out of my way to upset people, but if someone is offended by what I stand for, I don't want to work with them anyway. I'm not afraid to show who I am, and Propaganda is equally outspoken as an agency. We enjoy standing out and making our clients stand out too, and if that means being the underdog or fighting for the underdog, all the better.

I'd seen the light, and I was bravely and confidently marching towards it, knowing that it was the right thing to do. The changes we had made ensured that we had the right people and approach to work with clients at the C-suite level, not on one-off projects but as long-term partners for anything from two years to two decades. We wanted to deliver genuine value by selling great ideas, and now we had the gravitas to do just that.

There was no shortage of planners up north because many of the planners they were hiring in London were northerners anyway, so we had no problem recruiting them. We were the first agency outside of London to have a planning department, but it took around two years to get into our groove with the approach even though we had the right people in place. Like a new piece of software or a new-build house, there were bugs and issues to iron out – teething problems – and we were also offering a completely different type of service to prospects and clients who had never considered this way of doing things. It was bound to take a little time.

An important element of the planning approach is to ensure you are driven by the data rather than a desire to impress industry peers with award-winning creative ideas. We were focused on providing the best possible solutions for our clients, even if that meant doing nothing. A prime example of this was when we were hired by a British manufacturer to defend against a threat from overseas. While I have tried to give details where possible, when you're working with CEOs of large brands as a trusted board member, confidentiality comes with the territory, and I can't reveal the name of the company on this occasion.

Their product was ahead of its time when it launched, and it quickly became loved by its target market. It was something that they needed, and there were no alternative solutions. That changed when an American manufacturer tried to muscle into the UK market with a similar product. The British company was seriously concerned, and they asked us to conjure up a marketing solution.

After carrying out a ton of research and gathering lots of data, our advice was to do nothing. The brand was so well established in the UK that the name had almost become synonymous with its function in the same way that people refer to vacuum cleaners as 'Hoovers' or ball-point pens as 'Biros'. The Americans would have to throw millions at their campaign to make even a small dent in the market, and they'd soon conclude it wasn't worth the effort and turn their attention elsewhere. Customers loved the British product. There was no problem to fix. All the company needed to do was to sit tight because its brand was strong enough as it was. We advised them to stay confident and be brave. And the cost of that advice to sit tight and do nothing? Ten grand.

Other agencies would have mapped out a full creative brief to answer a problem that didn't exist. We had the confidence and courage to charge for our capacity to think and generate ideas, even if the result of that work was to recommend that they do nothing. I gave them that advice because it was the best course of action. It wasn't a plan that would ever win a design or campaign award and bring prestige to our company, but not only did that client not resent the spend, they loved us for the honest insight we'd given them.

## Brand is business, business is brand

Our approach was tactics-neutral. We were simply giving the right advice, not trying to push the client into a campaign that looked great but achieved nothing. All that glistens is not gold, as they say. We were paid for our thoughts. Propaganda is a thinking agency, and our job is to identify the thing that makes people love and buy from our clients; we then use that knowledge to help them grow.

Critics argued that the data-driven planning process was killing creativity. That's nonsense. You only have to look at the campaigns we have produced to see that there is no shortage of creativity here. The key difference is that we establish the facts first and build our creative plans based on that evidence, rather than based on assumptions. It's about producing creative that works, first and foremost.

Our planning product is called Brand Discovery™, and we charge for it because it's the most valuable work we do. It's pointless creating any campaigns without carrying out the discovery exercise first. That lays the foundations. Our discovery process is thorough and takes a minimum of three months. When we did it for ghd fifteen years ago, we charged £25,000. It was hugely effective – that company went from being perceived as a white goods manufacturer that people could take or leave to a global brand that their customers loved and wanted. Our fee was a drop in the ocean compared to the brand's long-term return on investment. These days, we charge anywhere from £60,000 to six figures.

By going down the discovery route, we were, by default, excluding ourselves from the pitch game. The discovery process takes three months. When you pitch, you have three weeks, a month at most, to come back with ideas. Those ideas are never going to be based on a process of acquiring deep knowledge before assumption. You haven't got the time to gather the knowledge you need, so the ideas you come up with won't be informed by much more than a toe-dip into what will inevitably be a small and non-representative section of the marketplace. History is littered with big brands that collapsed because they implemented such ill-thought out, rushed ideas.

The whole methodology (if there is one) of 'pitching' is to take a punt with an idea you already have or have come up with and hope that the business you're pitching to will buy it. Winning a pitch is a bit like winning the room with a side-splitting joke. The problem with that approach is that the funniest jokes are often the ones you get bored of telling (and others get bored of hearing) after a couple of weeks. The strongest brands are the ones that pass the test of time. Some of the brands that I grew up knowing are just as well known by today's children, and they'll probably still be around when they have grandchildren. These are not the funniest jokes in the room, but they are sophisticated enough to amuse the right audience for decades and perhaps even centuries to come, while their initially side-splitting counterparts are quickly forgotten.

Walking away from pitching created friction internally because it was a counterintuitive thing to do. It was natural to want to enter the race when prospects asked for pitches, and not doing so was nerve-wracking and required bravery. But I insisted that we were not going to contradict our discovery-first ethos, and that is something I have never looked back on. We get the work without pitching because we deliver results. The process is effective, and clients know that they've spent their money wisely because we are taking the time we would have spent pitching and using it to deliver genuine value.

## How do you rate an agency?

Despite what I said earlier, we do win plenty of awards – but not the inward-looking, narcissistic, 'let's pat each other on the back' industry recognition awards that other agencies rave about. The recognition we receive is not about how clever our photography was or an avant-garde approach to copywriting. We are internationally recognised consultants as measured against some of the leading strategists in the world. Our expertise and the results we have generated have led to us winning six Management Consultancies Association (MCA) awards, and we are a *Financial Times*-accredited consultant. Those are the kinds of awards we care about.

To get that type of respect and recognition, our processes and governance have to be just as sharp as the advice we offer. These are the credentials that get Propaganda a seat at the table in any boardroom, and we still score ten out of ten on creativity while delivering high-quality, well-thought out, award-winning strategies.

My advice for anyone looking for a branding agency would be this: have you seen their work before? Ignore any hype or industry awards for 'creativity'. What have they done? What *results* have they achieved? That's the most important measure of their usefulness, not the amount of billable time they've clocked up or their tenure. Who cares? Look at their output.

Propaganda has a growth mindset, so we are always learning. That said, I am proud of what we have achieved. We have produced viral brands, and that kind of outcome counts for more than anything. That's our purpose.

# SIX
# Quality Over Quantity

When Propaganda came to Leeds and I looked at all the other agencies operating in that space, I saw another set of village firms to beat. Different names, uniforms, and fighting styles, but it was warfare all the same – and I wasn't the least bit intimidated by any of them. The owner of one of those firms, Poulters, told me to my face that we wouldn't last five minutes. Those words stank of fear to me and just made me even more determined to show them who the new kings in town were.

We were outnumbered in every sense of the word – a small fish entering a big pond with plenty of much larger fish – but one thing I learned as a casual was not to care about numbers. One of the first casual crews to form in Scotland was Aberdeen's ASC (Aberdeen

Soccer Casuals). The city's oil industry had created significant wealth, so a lot of the young lads had easy access to expensive labels. The ASC grew rapidly, and they were always well turned out.

Despite their strength in numbers, whenever the ASC faced Edinburgh's Hibs (Hibernian) firm, they knew they were going to have a challenging time of it. Over the years, there hadn't been much between them until one occasion when only around thirty of the ASC turned up for a game. That's a small group, and especially tight for an away game, but they won that battle convincingly. So, less is sometimes more – but why?

## A team of calibre

Military leaders have always been aware of the principle of quality over quantity, and the world's most feared and respected special forces regiments operate in small numbers. A great example of this is our SAS (Special Air Service), which became internationally famous overnight in 1980 after a team of its elite soldiers stormed the Iranian Embassy to free twenty-one civilian hostages from a group of terrorists. They secured a successful outcome with excellent planning, courage, and the element of surprise. The main thing that differentiates units such as the SAS from other military teams is their efficiency. They achieve these kinds of outcomes by recruiting only the very best soldiers they can find, training them to an incredibly high standard across multiple disciplines, and devising detailed plans for every operation.

There are other advantages to using smaller units – they are less conspicuous, harder to detect, highly mobile, and have the advantage of stealth – but those advantages can only be effectively leveraged because of the calibre of every soldier in each unit. Plans depend on all operatives being disciplined enough to stay on track, mentally and physically fit enough to do what they need to do, and smart enough to adapt to sudden and unexpected changes. These people are few and far between, but they are out there. This was what I looked for when I came to recruit staff for Propaganda, because I wanted to build a stealthy, agile team that could get the job done right.

## Committed and organised – no runners

The reason the ASC was able to overpower Edinburgh's casuals with a much smaller crew was because of the calibre of the people who showed up that day. I am not suggesting for a moment that they were highly trained or even disciplined, but every one of them meant business. The larger the team, the more likely it is that some of them will just be there for the ride, neither fully committed nor particularly talented. Others would assume an easy victory and so wouldn't have the right mindset for the challenge.

There's an old saying that 'the bigger they are, the harder they fall,' and there's a lot of truth to it. A large but disorganised group of people of varying levels of ability will not be as efficient or effective as a small group of highly skilled, extremely focused people. The dead wood will get in the way of its talent, resulting in lots of action but no progress. In the case of the ASC, many of its members were classic cases of 'all the gear but no idea'. They looked the part, but they weren't effective fighters. Some of them will have been 'runners', lads who would run away as soon as the odds looked slightly less favourable.

But the thirty or so ASC members who travelled to Edinburgh that day would have been up for it. They were the most committed, loyal, and determined casuals in the crew, the kind of fighters who would stand their ground even when a serious beating looked inevitable. One of them could take on ten runners because the runners would run, and those who didn't would be ineffective because they'd be shitting themselves.

If you're wondering where I'm going with this, let me ask you this question: who would you rather have on your team, runners or fighters? That's a rhetorical question of course, because we all know the answer.

## No room for average

If I have learned anything during the thirty years that I have been running Propaganda, it's that while I am CEO, we're never going to have more than fifty staff.

The usual job of a business is to grow, and most companies are obsessed with growth, but it doesn't work for us. We have tried and succeeded on three occasions, once peaking at 120 staff, but do you know something? To be brutally honest, if I were a client, I would not have hired Propaganda during those periods.

In contrast, whenever there were fifty or fewer of us, I would hire us over any other agency every time, and I mean that literally. I did use us. A sarcastic idiot, who thought they were clever, once challenged me on this. They asked, 'If you're so fucking good at building brands, why haven't you built one of your own?' Putting aside that we were doing extremely well at building the Propaganda brand, I picked up the gauntlet they had thrown and founded the cruelty-free cosmetics brand, Illamasqua. I don't do things in half-measures and, by extension, neither does Propaganda. When I decide to do something, it has to be the best it can be, and I was determined to make sure Illamasqua started with a bang, got noticed, and won respect from the day of the launch. It was an ambitious project, to say the least, but one that we nailed – I will share more on that in a later chapter.

A major factor in why we don't go past fifty staff is how difficult it is to find staff who are good enough. I don't do average, and I don't employ average either. If you are looking for someone to do your books and fill in a tax return every year, average is probably adequate. An average data entry clerk might not be the quickest, but they may not need to be. There are plenty of other roles where those you hire can either do the job or they can't; there's no real need to excel. But there are other occupations and roles where average is not good enough. Imagine going for heart surgery and being told they hadn't got the best surgeon for the job, but the person on whom you were depending to save your life was average. That's an extreme example, of course, but no less true.

Propaganda is in the business of branding, and if you want someone who can do that well, you need much better than average. We exist to elevate our clients' brands to the point that those in their target market immediately identify with them and feel compelled to buy. Average can't do that. Average will not get you noticed. There are plenty of people who can write average copy, design average logos, plan average campaigns, and produce average brochures and other assets, but lack the courage or ability to come up with anything innovative, out there, or unique. They follow the crowd, stick with the tried and tested, and do what they do because that's what they were taught however many years ago when they were at college. Even those who start with an edge can lose it because they churn out ideas that were once outstanding but have become outdated. Laziness, fear, complacency. There are so many plausible explanations for someone average, but whichever way you flower it up, they're not producing the results and we don't want them on our team.

The problem, of course, is that no one ever turns up for an interview and tells you they're average. They come with carefully rehearsed presentations, lists of qualifications, and impressive stories to demonstrate how original and talented they are. It's only after contracts have been signed and they are drawing a salary that you realise the most creative things about them are their CVs.

Other agencies may be happy to accept what I call 'blaggers' and 'journeymen' on their teams, and they do. Perhaps they see it as a fact of life, one of the costs of growing a large team, but I won't stand for it. We only want the best.

## Splitting the wheat from the chaff

Every member of our team is genuinely creative, innovative, dedicated to their projects, and aware of all the other pieces in the jigsaw. They understand how the team works and how their output fits in with everyone else's. This might sound cliché, but they are genuinely driven by a passion for excellence because the pride they take in their work won't allow them to produce average. They're perfectionists. They want perfection because that's what makes them tick, and creating something that stands out because of its quality is far more important to them than personal glory and stories of big bonuses that they can share in their next job interview. Those things come automatically when projects succeed gloriously.

We use a highly sensitive 'average filter' to split the wheat from the chaff and so save time and effort. Hiring average not only limits a business's potential, it is also a costly mistake. Taking on the wrong people causes disappointment, letting them go is not pleasant, and then you have to start over with the recruitment process. I look for high-quality staff who will become long-term assets in the Propaganda team.

Our recruitment process looks pretty similar to everyone else's – right up to the point when contracts are signed, and they are about to start work. Looking superb on paper and performing well in interviews doesn't guarantee a career in our agency. Every successful candidate must pass a three-month trial period, and we're blunt about it. 'Well done. You've got the job. You have three months.' That's enough to put many people off – average people, certainly – but that's exactly what it's there to do. If the idea of a three-month probation period is too much for them to handle, that's a red flag. What are they afraid of – not being rewarded for mediocrity? I don't want people like that on our team.

At one time, only one in ten of those who accepted the challenge were kept on after the initial three-month trial period. We weren't playing, and we needed everyone to know that. This enabled us to attract the most ambitious and special individuals and, perhaps more importantly, show our prospects and clients that we were serious about being the best team in town.

## Look deeper

Business gurus will tell you that a high staff turnover is a red flag, and it can be. High turnover is bad news if you're losing your best people and don't understand why. High turnover is undesirable if it is a consequence of a toxic and unhappy working environment. High turnover is a dreadful predicament if it's causing people to steer clear of your organisation, so I can hardly blame the rest of the industry, especially in Leeds, for dismissing us as arrogant: 'You don't want to go there. They're shit to work for. Why do you think people are leaving?' Except for one thing – they were wrong. While they were putting us down, believing we were a dysfunctional organisation, three things were happening right under their noses.

Far from being put off by our high turnover, the best in the market were raising eyebrows and looking more closely. They recognised that people weren't leaving us, we were leaving them, and those who had what it took to stay *loved* working for us. Despite the best efforts of our detractors, the most talented people in our industry were increasingly seeing getting (and keeping) a job in our agency as a badge of success.

It's easy to look to the people leaving an organisation and listen to their complaints, but if you want to know what is really going on, speak to the ones who stay. The people staying on at Propaganda felt empowered and part of something bigger than 'nice creative'. They were making a difference, and they were anything but unhappy. At the time of writing, there are forty-five of us at Propaganda, half of whom have been here for at least fifteen years, including some who have been with our agency for a quarter of a century. Does that sound like a company that's 'shit' to work for?

Our policy was making us more attractive to our clients too. The first thing I would say to clients and prospects in business meetings was, 'If you talk to any other agency about us, they are going to tell you we have high staff churn. We don't. We have a rigorously policed trial period, which most candidates fail because they are not good enough. Once we've given them the chance, we pay no heed to their past and track record. We're interested in what they can do for our clients, not what they've done before. What that means for you is that you are getting the best service from the most talented branding experts in the industry.' Our clients loved us for it, and they still do.

The thing is, no matter what anyone says, every business owner knows what it is like to select the wrong candidate. One bad apple can cause a lot of rot, and for many businesses that don't have the appropriate clauses nailed down in their employment contracts, getting rid of unproductive staff can be a nightmare. I'd rather spend more time making sure I'm hiring the most innovative, creatively brave, and focused individuals than losing hours and days trying to expel those who aren't good enough. The latter need to go quickly. As cruel as it sounds, when a client hears that we have a policy that ensures the best service and shields them from poor performance, they understand and appreciate it. It's a bonus, not a disadvantage. A strength, not a weakness.

I fully accept that there was a boldness in our approach. Not arrogance (something our competitors accused us of) because that would imply that we thought we were so good, we didn't have to try. We were trying extremely hard, going to greater lengths than anyone else in our industry to ensure we had the most capable people on our team. We used a brutal but effective method to do that, and maybe it did put some clients off. Some would have bought into the idea that we were a shit company to work for. So what? That just meant they weren't right for us. What mattered was that those who were meant for us were hiring us, and the alignment was there from the start. That alignment led to some excellent outcomes, and even those who have since moved on have continued to succeed by following the branding principles that we put in place for them.

The beauty of our heavy filter recruitment approach, although not by design, was that no one else in Leeds saw us coming. They underestimated us because of their assumptions about what they perceived to be a weakness, and they failed to notice that the strongest candidates around wanted to join us. It was only when their clients started migrating to Propaganda because they weren't prepared to pay for mediocrity that the agencies in Leeds realised what had hit them. It was a stealthy approach. We are ruthless, and we are not for everybody, but we mean business, and the staff who stay know this.

We didn't have to create chaos behind enemy lines by sending over troublemakers to sabotage our competitors' efforts. They were doing a good enough job of that without our help, by taking on the people we wouldn't hire. Nine out of ten of the candidates we turned away ended up in the loving arms of those other agencies.

## The price of average

We entered the market in Leeds determined to make a name for ourselves and our clients. When we made that move, we were into our tenth year as a company and anything but a large agency. Leeds was full of giants, and we were surrounded by loads of well-established firms that had hundreds of staff. We didn't come to dabble, and as our list of clients grew – and they stayed with us – our competitors were paying the price of being average by having to pitch for everything and losing key clients and their best people. You can only pay that price for so long, and it was just a matter of time before, one by one, they started collapsing or significantly downsizing.

Ironically, one of the companies that had accused us of arrogance fell victim to their own arrogance. It was the reason they failed. If they had been paying attention, striving for excellence, and being more diligent in their approach to recruitment, they might have still been here today. I think the board at the time dismissed us as competitors. They were all acting like eighties ad men and yet the world had moved on... and this was the North, not London.

# SEVEN

# Kingmaking

The fact that we have stood the test of time and weathered many storms is a testament to the robustness of our approach. Once we embraced the planning methodology and established a foothold in the C-suite, we could finally stand shoulder-to-shoulder with our clients, and their fight became our fight. That's why we are now trusted to take the helm for massive brands – or at least have a firm hand on the wheel.

There's not enough space in this book to list every client we have worked with. However, there are a few notable case studies worth sharing here, starting with a product that was once considered so lowly that it fell into the category of 'white goods', namely a ceramic styling iron that went on to become a global brand: ghd.

Hair irons had existed for decades – my mother had several versions of them lying around the house when I was growing up – but there was no emotional attachment. Consumer loyalty was to the lowest price – they couldn't care less about the brand. They may as well have been buying car insurance. When was the last time you heard anyone say how delighted they were to pay for that? Consumers were buying the cheapest product and keeping it until it broke.

## ghd – a blueprint for brand building

It is sixteen years since we worked with ghd, but we still get enquiries from companies asking if we can 'do a ghd' for them. There is a saying that good work breeds work, but I think the case of ghd proved that pioneering work can continue to generate enquiries and sales for decades.

The product was originally manufactured by a firm in Korea. After failing to get any interest in the US, it landed in the hands of a British entrepreneur: Robert Powls. He gave it to his wife to try and she was delighted with it, declaring that she was having a 'good hair day', or 'GHD' for short. Soon after, Robert brought in two co-directors and ghd was launched.

I am told our work with ghd is still considered one of the best blueprints for developing a strong brand from a standing start in a sector dominated by giants. The seeds for this collaboration were sown when I met one of the brand's shareholders, Martin Penny, at a business event. I can't remember what I said to him to leave such a strong impression but when he approached me a year later, he said that my perspective on branding had resonated so much that he'd decided there and then that he would hire me if the opportunity arose.

Given that ghd went on to become our biggest client to date, with a retainer worth £166,000 per month, you will be shocked to learn that I wasn't in attendance at the first two meetings. I didn't go to the first because my attitude was along the lines of, *It's a hair styler – I'll let someone else take that meeting*. When they approached me the second time, I had to cancel because I was invited to a shoot at Balmoral on the same day. Putting aside that I'd never even handled a shotgun, let alone fired one, how could I turn down an invitation to the Queen's estate? That turned out to be a life-changing event in more ways than one because I went there, took the life of a grouse, instantly regretted it, and vowed never to take the life of an animal again. Fortunately, ghd's directors were determined enough to give me a third chance, and this time I accepted.

At my first meeting with them, we heard about how the flagship product was already delivering noticeable growth, with no marketing. ghd's unique selling point was the type of ceramic plate they were using. Once the owners had convinced us that they were the first to market with this game-changing technology and of the impact it would have on fast and effective hair styling, our interest was piqued.

One of the three directors, Gary Douglas, explained the brief:

> 'We've been in business for eighteen months, and we've made a lot of money. We've sold around £3.5m of these products to salons in London, with no infrastructure and no real marketing spend. More than half of that was profit, which we've split three ways between us.
>
> 'The problem we've got is that there are many brands, far bigger than us, coming into this sector, and we know we can't compete with them. We accept we have got lucky here. Over the next couple of months, we are prepared to throw about £50,000 at it.'

They wanted to make the most of the time they had left to earn each of them another half a million or so and double what they'd already had out of the business.

If we were going to work with these guys, we were going to do it right. As ghd had approached us just as we'd decided we were switching to the planning model, I went back to them and asked for £25,000, half of the budget they'd offered, to begin the process that would tell me what they should be doing. The three directors agreed, and that leap of faith turned out to be one of the best decisions they'd ever made. It also proved to be a pivotal moment for us at Propaganda, as ghd became our first-ever Brand Discovery client.

## What did we learn?

Many brands had noticed the growth that ceramic styling irons were achieving in the hair and beauty sector, and an astounding forty-two of them launched in competition with ghd within a short period. These included the hi-fi brand Bang & Olufsen, the celebrity underwear model Caprice, and electrical big hitters such as Braun, Clairol, and BaByliss. They all wanted to seize the opportunity to sell a styling iron of comparable quality on the high street for a fraction of the price. They were also going to use their buying power to purchase their product at a much lower cost price than a company trading only a few million could expect to.

On the face of it, this congested and changing marketplace sounded an early, very loud death knell for ghd. We urgently needed to understand what made ghd different and special so that we could counter the threat. We already knew that ghd wasn't retailing directly to the consumer but, during discovery, we learned they were selling to around 250 salons in London. Robert Powls was a stylist himself, and he believed the product should be in the capital's best salons. We set out to speak to these salons, hoping to hear about why they thought ghd styling irons were brilliant so we could tap into that knowledge and bottle that brilliance within a brand message. This stage of discovery led to two valuable insights.

First, our assumptions about why salons were purchasing ghd products couldn't have been further from the truth. While salon owners were impressed with the quality of the product and the results, it was the transformational effect that ghd had on their salon revenues that built their emotional connection and loyalty to the brand. With a retail price of £130, selling the ghd irons was a significant new revenue stream for them – it represented business growth with no need for more staff or space. They were making more from the sale of a single ghd styling iron than they were from five haircuts, and the transaction took seconds instead of hours in the chair. For the business owners, it meant their first Porsche Boxster (apologies for the cliché), an additional foreign holiday, or other luxury items. Frankly, selling ghd was life-changing for many of them.

Second, stylists carry huge personal gravitas and attract loyalty from their clients. You can see that when a stylist leaves a salon – their customers often go with them. Put simply, the stylist's word is God, and if they say a product is the best, no one questions them. Salon owners became influencers for ghd long before the term was being used as it is now, and their recommendations were key to sales success.

We could see how the competitive threat was not only going to directly affect ghd but also the profits the salon owners had been enjoying. We could also see how this knowledge could be leveraged to encourage them to go the extra mile in promoting ghd to their customers.

Our consumer groups gleaned further insight. One group comprised people who had bought ghd, and a control group had heard of ghd but not used its products. When we relayed their feedback to ghd's directors, they took great pleasure in saying that we must have confused the two groups because the people who had not used the product sounded just like the ones who had – both groups were singing its praises. Someone rightly pointed out that the product's status and following was almost religious – it was being evangelised by people who had no direct experience of it.

## From insight to action – leveraging knowledge to generate exponential growth

The discovery process delivered enough rich insight for us to formulate a plan to mobilise the support of salon owners and produce an effective advertising campaign.

First, we advised ghd to approach the salon owners with a warning that the market was changing rapidly and suggesting that it was in their best interest to denounce other brands and champion ghd's product. In return for their support, ghd would deliver increased footfall to participating salons through its advertising campaign.

For the second part of our plan, we asked ghd to give us £300,000 – on top of the £25,000 they had already paid for Brand Discovery – for us to put them on television. While the media budget was small in terms of driving awareness, we knew this would demonstrate our commitment to the salon owners (as this would be the first professional-only product to go on television) and we would reap the rewards in their increased loyalty and ongoing recommendations.

The directors agreed, and we produced an advertisement that drew on ghd's cult-like, almost religious appeal. The campaign focused on religious iconography, and we sparked a striking must-have new look for women in the process – poker-straight hair. Adopting an anti-celebrity approach, the ghd advertisement featured girl-next-door, everyday women who, transformed by ghd, became 'Urban Angels. Made, not born.' From then on, all ghd advertisements had a religious undertone or theme, such as 'the Gospel of ghd'. Another key part of the message was that ghd was 'only available in the finest salons.'

Our campaigns covered all bases – a product that transformed regular people into supermodels, a must-buy that was almost a rite of passage for any woman who was serious about making every day a good hair day, and a tool that no stylist worth their salt would be seen without.

One year later, ghd sales hit £8 million, flying in the face of the expectation that the brand would be crushed by the plentiful opposition and vanish from the marketplace. What followed can only be described as exponential growth. Another twelve months later, they reached £18 million, then £36 million, and finally £60 million – which is when the directors sold the brand.

The success of the advertising campaign is testament to the power of discovery. It gave the directors the confidence to invest in it, something discoveries continue to do for brands to this day. The rigour of the discovery process gives clients the belief and courage to invest in something bold.

While sales were booming and the money was rolling in for the directors who had thought the brand's days were numbered, something equally magnificent was happening for us. Girls were fighting over ghd carrier bags, and such was the enthusiasm for, loyalty to, and cult status of the brand, that it rubbed off on Propaganda as ghd's outsourced marketing department. I was made the brand's marketing director, sitting on the board. When I took my team into a nightclub to do a promo, people were approaching us as though we were rockstars. It was phenomenal. We also noticed something else: the more ghd charged for its products, the more they sold.

What had started as a London-centric product became a globally loved brand, and we launched it in Europe, Australia, and America. I was spending three days a week with ghd and only a couple at Propaganda, but at this point the two were inseparable. They were our biggest client by a country mile. I knew I was breaking every rule in the book by being so invested in ghd, but I was going with the flow. It felt right. One thing I hadn't anticipated while I was on the board was the inevitable flood of approaches from venture capitalists (VCs). There was money to be made and interest from potential buyers. By year four or five, I was delivering presentations to one VC after another.

## You can't put a price on principles

When ghd's first VC invested in the company, I was naïve about the process. When their first directive was to cut back on branding, I thought it was singularly the most ridiculous advice I'd ever heard. The product cost the same to produce as many others on the market. The reason ghd could sell its product for five times as much as everyone else back then was brand.

Ignoring my advice, they cut the marketing spend for twelve months to maximise profits and then sold it to another VC a year after that for a mammoth number. In the cold light of day, from a purely business perspective, I can't criticise them for what they did, but I despised them for risking a brilliant brand for the sake of forcing short-term profitability. The brand was impacted and lost its edge for a few years, and I wasn't comfortable with that. There is more to life than money, and I take pride in the brands I help to grow.

I was still a shareholder in the new VC-owned business, and they expected me to be delighted. 'You're going to make so much money. What's your problem?' they asked. The world of venture capitalism is soulless, and I didn't build Propaganda only to sell my soul for dollars. That was the problem, and I couldn't live with much of what they wanted to do. It was an affront to my professionalism, and I felt conflicted. The matter eventually resolved itself after an incident in the boardroom put fire in my belly and brought my warrior spirit back to the fore.

In one of the first board meetings that I sat in on, one of the newly appointed board members behaved worse than a bully towards a female colleague in full view of the rest of the board. He spoke to her like dirt, and there was no way I was going to allow his uncalled-for, humiliating attack to go unchallenged. The dressing down I gave to that silly old sod in front of the board won't be forgotten until the guy is well into retirement, and it sealed my fate where my and Propaganda's involvement with ghd were concerned.

Within a matter of days, both Propaganda and I resigned from ghd, although I remained bound by the non-compete terms of gardening leave for the next twelve months. Shortly after, other agencies got wind of what had happened and contacted me to praise me for my courage. By their own admission, they could have been shat on from a great height, and they still would not have resigned. Some may say I was foolish for doing what I did, but I regret not one word of what I said or my decision to pull away from ghd, although I was sad to say goodbye to the brand that I'd played such a vital part in building. My principles are worth more than a £1 million-a-year contract. The bullying and the shabby attitude towards branding, driven by greed, made the situation intolerable for me, and nothing could be said, done, or offered to make me stay on the board. Everyone did incredibly well out of ghd, including me, but I am not greedy and my principles were worth more to me. However, even though at the time I was making a big sacrifice, the decision to leave has given me tenfold returns through additional work and new clients. You could call it karma. When you do the right thing, you get paid back eventually.

During Propaganda's tenure at ghd, no other styling iron brand got close to them. While they could charge more and still sell more, other brands couldn't get a foot in the door, even when selling their product for a fraction of the price. ghd were in a league of their own. From one of the fastest-growing businesses in 2005 to being recognised for innovation, they were cleaning up and collecting silverware as though it were going out of fashion.

For every award we won, I would step up with ghd's owners to collect the spoils. Propaganda's successful collaboration with the brand led to my being invited to Sir Richard Branson's house for the *Sunday Times* fastest-growing business award. I also picked up another accolade at Highgrove House, where I met the then Prince of Wales, for planning a ghd campaign to raise awareness of breast cancer.

I don't think it would be an exaggeration or arrogant to say the branding work we did with ghd was far superior to anything the company has done since. Now owned by COTY Group, ghd still hasn't lost its cult following and will be a source of pride for me and Propaganda for many years to come.

One brand did eventually appear, out of nowhere, as a true challenger to ghd. Within its launch period, it took over a thousand salons from ghd. That brand still exists today. That brand is Cloud Nine, and we were behind its launch. We commenced the work on the day we were released from the competitive restrictions on our contract with ghd.

## A brand of our own – Illamasqua

In the aftermath of the ghd situation, one of the three directors and I started to fall out. He did what many people have done: let success go to his head and colour his perception of events.

Propaganda are kingmakers. Our role is to make our clients hugely successful. It should never be about us, how cool we are, how funky our campaigns are, or how much money we make. We focus on building brands into market leaders. It is excellent when clients honestly acknowledge our contribution, and we appreciate it, but it's not written into our contracts that they must.

One of the guys at ghd had convinced himself that our contribution had been minimal. 'We'd have been this successful without you,' he had the audacity to claim. It was around that time that the other smart arse I mentioned had taunted me, effectively challenging me to start a brand of my own. These remarks tipped it, and I was ready to enter a new battle, this time to fight for my reputation and the reputation of Propaganda. If someone throws the gauntlet in my direction, especially one with my name written all over it, I won't hesitate to pick it up.

So I set myself a challenge: to start a brand from scratch in a totally new to me market and make it into a market leader within three years. I asked two of my most trusted associates to do a bit of digging and suggest a suitable sector for me to have a go at. They both came back with the same conclusion – makeup.

Makeup is one of, if not the, toughest sectors on the planet to penetrate because the market is dominated by a cartel: L'Oréal, Estée Lauder, and two 'smaller' brands…Chanel and Louis Vuitton. Brands that have succeeded in the makeup sector have usually had to invest at least £25 million, twenty-five years of marketing, or both. I was going to create a leading brand in the makeup sector and do it with £5 million of my own money over five years. It was an insanely ambitious project, almost impossible to achieve, and that only made me more determined to go for it.

## Game on – breaking into the makeup sector

I'd set the bar as high as possible, and I need to plan out the steps to get there, starting with bringing together the right people to help me. To have any chance of success, I would need the strongest possible team, so I hand-picked the most capable individuals from the one I had built for ghd.

The next step was discovery, and I threw myself into the market to absorb as much as I could. Before my casual days, I had occasionally worn makeup as a goth, inspired by my goth girlfriends who used it to create the sexiest look on the planet and Dave Vanian of The Damned who, I'd argue, wore it better than any woman I've ever known.

My team and I visited tens upon tens of beauty halls across the UK, and the pattern that quickly emerged was the consistent use of the term 'professional', which they deployed early in their messaging, often in the first line. When I asked frontline staff to explain what they meant by the term, many didn't understand the question and those who did would say things like, 'Bobbi Brown is a professional makeup artist,' which seemed irrelevant to me. You wouldn't want an F1 supercar to be manufactured by Lewis Hamilton, would you? Understanding how to apply makeup and knowing how to manufacture it are completely different things. The owner being a makeup artist didn't justify describing the product as professional. Baffling though this common practice was, it provided me with a clue as to how I could create a brand that was genuinely different from all the rest.

We found a German company called Kryolan that was manufacturing top-of-the-range cosmetics and had a remarkable backstory – the kind of story that brands are built on. What's more, Kryolan was producing a unique product that was genuinely worthy of being called professional.

In the 1920s, theatre companies were under pressure to up their game because of the rise of Hollywood and the film industry. Actors found themselves in a different world where they had to focus on acting under the guidance of directors while specialists took care of everything else, from the lighting to the set design and, of course, makeup. This was a highly technical challenge.

Makeup had to be heat-resistant so it wouldn't melt under the glare of the lights, and there was a demand for precise colours to ensure historical accuracy for productions such as *Cleopatra*. Ordering 'green' eye-shadow wasn't good enough anymore. It had to be chartreuse green rather than 'green' from an era when the Pantone Colour System hadn't yet been conceived.

A young German man called Arnold Langer rose to the challenge and began producing makeup that met a high enough spec to be used by professionals. He went on to found Kryolan, selling makeup to the film industry, television companies, opera houses, and the theatre companies the idea had emerged from. Kryolan still carries as much weight in those sectors today as it did a century ago, and the brand is synonymous with high-quality professional makeup. A brand doesn't become professional simply because professionals use it. Only a brand designed to meet the unique needs of professionals can genuinely be called professional.

When we discovered Kryolan, we also noticed that there was no way for consumers to get their hands on its products, and that presented us with an open goal to aim at. We had the perfect product, a niche opportunity to offer it to consumers, and this product could be accurately described as professional. All I had to do was find Arnold and strike a deal.

Via a translator, we asked Arnold if we could openly use Kryolan formulas and declare an association with the brand. By explicitly stating that we were using its products and making them available to the public for the first time, we would leverage Kryolan's backstory to make an impact and get noticed quickly. We'd also be exposing dozens of other brands for falsely describing their products as professional. As Illamasqua was to be a cruelty-free brand, we had to ensure that Arnold would be happy to tweak Kryolan products accordingly. He gave us the green light on all fronts, and Illamasqua was go.

## A brand is born

The name Illamasqua came about by blending 'illusion' with 'masquerade' – highlighting the creative use of makeup to transform appearances, and adding the elements of mystery and theatricality. Illamasqua celebrates self-expression, individuality, and bold, artistic makeup looks. More than that, it lives up to its reputation as professional makeup.

Even before we had a branded prototype in its Illamasqua packaging, we'd successfully pitched it to Selfridges on Oxford Street, the biggest beauty door in the world. We were given the largest launch space they'd ever offered a makeup brand because they thought our idea was cool. Rather than following the usual monotone dull customer interactions we'd seen from other brands on those many visits to beauty halls up and down the country, we decided to make it all a show. Every day was a performance for Illamasqua, with energetic music, striking lighting, beautifully made-up drag queens with 12-inch heels, which we called 'creatures of the night' (recruited from talent-spotting expeditions to some of the underground clubs of the capital), along with many other theatrical staff, all of whom were allowed to express themselves freely. A phrase that I put at the heart of Illamasqua was that it is 'makeup for your alter ego.' We asked these people to bring their alter egos to work every day, and they showed up magnificently.

When we launched, we'd heard from our contact at Selfridges that someone senior was singing our praises: 'This is what I expect from brands on this shop floor. They are delivering theatre, not just products.'

It was the norm for brands to offer their products to high-profile individuals for free to gain more publicity and elevate their brand through association. We wouldn't do that, and we didn't have to. Illamasqua became an instant hit with A-listers such as Vicky McClure MBE, Boy George, and Amy Winehouse, amongst scores of other celebrities who were all happy to pay for the product. I took a call from Courtney Love in Malibu, who ordered three of everything – around 800 SKUs including eyeliners, blushers, lipsticks, foundations, and nail varnishes – at a cost of thousands of pounds, and one of my childhood heroes, Adam Ant, used to spend days at a time in the Illamasqua offices because he loved our brand so much.

## Not your average growth

Illamasqua took the fashion world by storm, and everyone wanted to write about it. Within three years of its launch, *Vogue* magazine heralded Illamasqua as 'the most significant brand in makeup for twenty-five years.' As word of our revolutionary brand spread around the globe, we received enquiries from far and wide, including Australia, where we launched an expensive roll-out through the retailer MYER. We even collaborated with our late Queen's funeral parlour, Levertons, where wealthy people could preorder their makeup for the afterlife!

Our commitment to producing a cruelty-free professional makeup brand added to Illamasqua's soul and strengthened its connection with its loyal fanbase. Never one to compromise on principles, when I became concerned about the rise of Donald Trump, I openly declared that we would not sell Illamasqua to Trump supporters. As you can imagine, this led to death threats. Trump supporters even hijacked my mobile number and Twitter feed to carry out an orchestrated campaign to defame me, using tactics that the now-convicted criminal is well known for. This included researching and sharing my past life as a football hooligan with my various business audiences – which wasn't a problem as I had never made a secret of any of it. Far from worrying me, I thought it was exciting.

My stance on Trump and his supporters also had its own fans, and we attracted lots of positive attention from Al Jazeera. More than that, it helped us to grow in a way we couldn't have predicted. It was a brave move. It was a move that backed my principles, and yet again, it demonstrated that when I back my principles, good things happen. Although sales in the middle belt of America sank, they exploded in the east and west, particularly along the East Coast. The net effect was the type of growth that we didn't have the money to achieve by other more conventional means.

Every time we got into a new department store, such as Bloomingdale's in the US, we had to pay costs towards the stand – a fee to compensate the store for the use of space, staff on the stands, and other expenses – so I had to look for an investor to support our continued growth. That led to a partnership with Joe Corré, founder of the underwear brand Agent Provocateur. Illamasqua was eventually acquired by THG PLC (formerly The Hut Group) in a deal worth close to £20 million in 2017, just nine years after it launched.

Apart from putting the critics in their place and proving our value as brand builders, putting my own money on the line taught me more about branding, and in a shorter time frame, than I could have learned any other way. It's easy to spend other people's money in the quest to grow a brand, but when it's your own, you learn what it feels like to be the client. Building

Illamasqua was a tough ride but also one of the most fun and adventurous projects of my career.

## From truckers to retail enablers – Clipper Logistics

Steve Parkin is one of many people who became aware of Propaganda, and me, through the work we did for ghd. With humble beginnings, having started his working life in the coal mines, he has supreme confidence and self-belief. We shared similar pasts – I think he would also be open and honest about his own courtship with the darker side of football at Leeds United – so the two of us gelled quickly. There was never a shortage of things to talk about, and we would reminisce for hours at a time if left unchecked. Our friendly conversations took over at least half of most meetings, much to the enjoyment and surprise of many of the others sitting with us. However, as is the case with all great businesspeople, he had a serious, single-minded side and when our discussions turned to how to grow his company, his vision was clear, and it was ambitious.

This man was intent on steering the world of logistics away from its long-held self-portrayal as the kind of business that simply owns trucks. The whole logistics scene at the time was lorry-obsessed, characterised by pissing contests typically focused on how many lorries they owned or how good their fleet livery looked, and the talk was more about lorries and warehouses than it was about consumers. Steve was determined to change all of that and achieve a burning ambition along the way – to float Clipper on the London Stock Exchange.

When I first met Steve in Brighouse in 2008, it was in a fairly grubby office, which I hope he doesn't mind me saying. It was back in the days when you'd have the odd 'girly calendar' on the wall, everyone smoked and no one thought anything of it – a different world from the one we live in today. Even describing itself as a logistics company was progressive because only a few years earlier, it had been calling itself a haulage business or haulier.

Steve, like many of our clients past and present, instinctively understood the power of brand. I clearly remember his succinct brief: 'We're the biggest logistics brand that nobody has heard of. I know we've got something special, but I can't define it.' In pursuit of his ambition and despite the economic downturn, the loss of several major customers due to bankruptcy, and the disapproval of a number of his board, he commissioned a Brand Discovery. He had balls.

While the rest of the world was evolving, Clipper belonged to a sector that had been left behind. Probably the most glamourous topic of conversation was the Eddie Stobart trucks, which were famously given the names of female celebrities such as Twiggy (the model), Tammy (Wynette), Dolly (Parton), and Suzi (Quattro).

That was about as exciting as things got in the 'logistics' industry.[7]

Working with Steve, we changed all of that, and Clipper remained an account of Propaganda's for fifteen years. I often consider what made the relationship as successful as it was, and I've boiled it down to three points:

1. Our direct relationship with Steve and his senior team – working closely together, day in, day out, aligned on business goals.

2. A complete lack of procrastination – we had a 'build it and they will come' mentality that powered the delivery of our plans.

3. Insight – without fail, we refreshed and retested our strategy every eighteen months, undertaking a new review of the market and customer landscape. It was a truly powerful cocktail and pivotal to our success.

The rise of Clipper was coruscating not only because of the dazzling growth in its turnover but also because of how it operated and the problems it solved. It became the blueprint that everyone wanted to follow and was eventually acquired by GXO in America for just shy

---

7. Illustrating how times have changed, Eddie Stobart has since expanded the tradition to include names with connections to drivers or to commemorate long-serving employees, and the company now features a much more diverse range of lorry names from around the globe.

of a billion pounds – a sector-breaking multiple. The transformation of this Leeds-based haulier into a global logistics firm par excellence and its meteoric rise and acquisition put Clipper Logistics in the spotlight, and some of that bright light fell on us.

The work that we did for Clipper was real consumer thinking in a business-to-business (B2B) environment; we dared to be different, to break the mould, and violate boring sector codes. We collaborated with Clipper to understand what their client's problems truly were. An example of that was recognising that the job was not to acquire lots of lorries or boast about working through the night. The job was to enable retail. That was why Clipper existed and the only reason anyone ever hired a logistics firm – to help them retail effectively.

It was this repositioning that truly set Clipper apart from everyone else in its sector, and it was based on a mantra to put the customer's needs front and centre. This mantra had sat within the business for years, although Clipper's repositioning only launched in the latter days and during the build-up to its eventual exit to GXO.

One of the great customer-focused things we did at Clipper was to create a sub-brand called Boomerang. This came off the back of an insight that the single most challenging problem faced by retailers, accelerated by the growth of e-commerce, was the growing issue of returns. Returns were mostly not thought about until they happened, which was fine for the odd occurrence here and there but became an increasingly significant issue when they became large in scale and there was no infrastructure to deal with them. As a retailer grew and sales increased, so too would the number of returns, until it hit a critical mass and the ensuing bottleneck would rip the heart out of many of the positive financial assumptions made, based on a daily profit and loss mentality. There was a spectre of returns out there, completely unaccounted for. They were costing companies a fortune to process, much more than businesses could afford, because there was no simple mechanism for handling them.

Retailers needed a method for dealing with returns more efficiently and cost-effectively. Clipper were super clever and developed that system and process, and we were just as smart in launching it to the market as a powerful unique selling point. The brand that we came up with still exists today – like the Australian instrument it's named after, Boomerang is all about the art of returns.

When we launched Boomerang, the sector went crazy for it. It created a buzz. Everyone was happy – Steve, me, the clients using Boomerang – and new business was flooding in. Once the headache of inefficiently processed returns hit profits to the extent that they were causing sleepless nights for financial directors, they'd say, 'I want Clipper in here.' They had a need, a problem they could not solve – how to handle the returns without haemorrhaging money – and Clipper had the solution.

With our help, Clipper, in a consumer-led way, managed to create a sub-brand that played into the hearts and minds of the financial directors, people with the power and will to make quick decisions. Boomerang multiplied the success of the business across every single measure – financial, gravitas, and customer loyalty. They were the darlings of their industry, and everywhere we went, the Clipper story began to have the same effect as the ghd story. In the same way that business-to-consumer (B2C) companies had been asking us to 'do a ghd' for them, B2B businesses started asking us to 'do a Clipper'. The irony is that we don't acknowledge those classifications (B2B and B2C). We believe in and adopt the principle of 'business to people' and apply it regardless of how a client is categorised. We don't feel that any of our B2B strategies have been second-rate in the way that B2B is normally accepted as being when compared to consumer marketing. The assumption that B2B marketing is inevitably unexciting is nonsense. Most of the time, we are simply bringing consumer thinking to clients who introduce themselves as B2B. But not every time...

## EIGHT
# Polish It Brightly

It shouldn't all be about money. While I was at Illamasqua, I had a flat in the village of Lindley in Huddersfield. It had an unusual structure, and one of its walls was twice as high as the others. Thanks to a company that could make anything into wallpaper, the tallest wall of my flat featured a 22-foot-tall image of a girl whose photograph we had taken at the Whitby Goth Festival. She was what you would call a 'cyber-goth'. The effect was striking, and so was everything else about the flat. I had created a highly stimulating workplace where I could focus on all things Illamasqua. It was almost a homage to the method-acting mindset of immersing oneself in a role, except my flat became a shrine to the world of creative makeup artistry and even more so the subcultures that inspired it.

It was this flat that I retreated to when I needed to write some Illamasqua copy, calling for women to wear makeup more boldly than the other brands were giving them permission to, and for men to rediscover the art of using it. We know consumers are influenced by the branding messages they receive, which means their possibilities are limited by how imaginative the branding industry is. Before ripped jeans became a thing, what did people do with their ripped jeans? Throw them out? I wanted Illamasqua's consumers to express themselves fully, without fear, and I wanted men to rediscover the wearing of makeup – if you look back at history, men and women were at least level pegging with makeup and certainly in many French courts, men were outdoing women.

While working, I often left the television on at a low volume to provide some background noise. It is no word of a lie that no sooner had I finished penning the copy than the news broke that a young couple, Sophie Lancaster and Rob Maltby, had both ended up in comas after being subjected to a severe beating from a feral group of teenage boys who chose to attack them because of the way they looked. At the time, they were both heavily made up, with facial piercings and dyed hair, and you can imagine how they may have been dressed. I believe the boys who set upon them simply felt threatened because of their own insecurities.

While Rob woke from his coma, Sophie never did, sadly, and passed away. After I heard the news, a shiver went down my spine. I had just crafted a call to action from my brand, encouraging more people to live like Rob and Sophie, and yet they had paid the ultimate price for simply existing that way. My brain quickly moved to whether my actions would cause others to meet the same fate, and I felt a strong sense of responsibility to insure against that possibility or, at the very least, to do something to balance things out.

## The Sophie Lancaster Foundation

Sophie's mum, Sylvia, was visiting Huddersfield a few weeks later for a memorial event, one of many that were taking place. I managed to speak to her. It wasn't easy. These things never are. I explained how I had come to hear about Sophie just as I had been writing about self-expression, and I shared my desire to help build something, anything – an organisation, or even a movement – to help prevent attacks like those inflicted on Sophie and her boyfriend from ever happening again. Someone close to Sophie, while sitting at her bedside, had come up with the slogan 'Stamp Out Prejudice, Hatred and Intolerance Everywhere' – an acrostic that spells out Sophie's name. If Illamasqua were looking for a collaboration, then this one was meant to be, and I wanted to help honour the spirit of those words.

During that conversation with Sylvia, I offered two things: for Illamasqua to fund the establishment of a charity, and the (free of charge) services of Propaganda to promote it. This led to the launch of The Sophie Lancaster Foundation, which adopted 'Stamp Out Prejudice, Hatred and Intolerance Everywhere' as its slogan. The charity strives to achieve its mission by 'teaching the importance of tolerance and inclusivity...stimulating and encouraging conversations about prejudice,' and 'celebrating difference, music and individuality.'[8] It spreads its message of tolerance and understanding in prisons, schools, festivals, and anywhere where it can have a positive effect on hearts and minds.

I am immensely proud of my involvement with the formation and launch of The Sophie Lancaster Foundation, although I ought to add that, with a heavy heart, I had to attend Sylvia's funeral in 2022. My spirits were lifted a little when three of the four people who delivered eulogies chose to mention my contribution. It dawned on me that Sylvia must have shared with these people just how vital my role was, at least in the early days. Knowing that I helped make a difference is something I will reflect on as a real career high. Money can pay bills and buy nice things, but to know you have touched hearts and made a difference is priceless.

The creative work we did for Sophie came about through a conversation we'd had with Sylvia where we asked her what it was like for Sophie to live in a

---

8. The Sophie Lancaster Foundation, www.sophielancasterfoundation
.com, accessed November 2024

small Northern town. We were told that every time she went out with her boyfriend or with her friends, they could expect a torrent of abuse. People would often just shout, 'Oi, you weirdo,' or 'You freak', or 'You mosher,' and this was on the polite end of the spectrum of abuse. We repurposed those words for a line that now adorns merchandise from the foundation and is, I would estimate, worn by tens of thousands of people around the globe on any one day: 'Weirdo. Mosher. Freak. If only they'd stopped at the name-calling.' It proves that sometimes our job isn't to change things or be creative for the sake of it. Sometimes it is just to listen, and the most creative thing to do is to have the sense not to change it. Later, Catherine Smyth, the first journalist to attend the scene where Sophie and Rob were viciously attacked in Bacup, Lancashire, adopted the same line for the title of her book.[9] More proof of the power of words.

## A lasting legacy

One of the things that Sylvia gave me was a framed picture of Sophie. Although I never met her, I feel as though I know her because she has been so much in my thoughts for so many years, and that framed photo seems to follow me around. Even while drafting this book, she's been with me most of the time, her photo perched on the edge of my desk in my home office.

---

9.  C Smyth, *Weirdo Mosher Freak: The murder of Sophie Lancaster* (self-published, 2020)

We also produced a film for Sophie and again, as is Propaganda's way, we showed that when you push yourself to do great work, not only can it get results, but it can also achieve the impossible. In our case, this meant managing to get an advertisement on MTV without paying for media space. One of the channel's executives saw the film, appreciated the message and the creativity, and chose to broadcast it. To get noticed by a company that must be asked to run ads ten times a day, every day, by people around the globe, shows how powerful that film was.

The film featured music from a band called Portishead. The track was a perfect match for the video and, again, guess what: there were no royalties. We didn't have to pay a penny. They gave us the track. In fact, many people offered their time and expertise to that film for free not only because of the horrific events that had inspired it but also because of the power of a great idea and the creativity that went into the project.

My former partner Joe Corré had a great saying, one which captures his and my style of brand building beautifully, and it is that sometimes you need to polish something so brightly that it radiates and attracts attention and people are drawn to it. If you don't have the money to bring them to it through traditional means like advertising, use what money and skill you have to polish it as brightly as you can. In the world of branding, this is a great analogy for how to outthink rather than outspend your competition.

# NINE

# GenM – Much More Than A Business

The co-founder of GenM was someone I was destined to work with. I first met Heather Jackson around three decades ago when Propaganda was in its infancy and we were operating from an office in Holmfirth, a picturesque village in Huddersfield famous for being where the television series *Last of the Summer Wine* was filmed. It is a lovely place in the middle of the most beautiful countryside, and I am fortunate to live only twenty minutes away. I spend a lot of time in the village, not least because it is home to The Picturedrome, an old picture house that has been converted into a venue where bands – many of whom are on my watch list – can perform.

A few doors down from our office was the studio and shop of Ashley Jackson, a highly acclaimed landscape artist who grew up in Barnsley before settling in Holmfirth, where he became well known in so much that his works adorned the walls of people with deep pockets and expensive taste. He often appeared on television and hosted his own show, *Ashley Jackson's Painting Britain*, which aired for many years, where he would take semi-professional and amateur artists to his beloved moors above Holmfirth and teach them how to paint in his distinctive and moving style. Our office was less than a stone's throw from this local celebrity.

Ashley was a genuine, down-to-earth person – unsurprising for someone coming from Barnsley. We developed a friendly rapport, often popping into each other's premises to say hello and have a chat, which is how I first met his daughter Heather. To this day, I often joke with Heather that my early impression was of Ashley coming to our office with this young girl in tow – a slightly skewed view given that, without asking a lady her age, I know there are not too many years between us.

Heather later reappeared, in my career and in hers, on a couple of occasions that I would term as false starts. On one of these, we sat in a room and talked about potentially exploring a licensing agreement regarding some of Ashley's paintings and a fabrics business that I was consulting for. Nothing came of that meeting. The second time Heather popped up on my radar was when she introduced a project to Propaganda through her partner at the time. I can't remember the details of that collaboration, but our paths crossing again was another sign that we would inevitably find a way to work together on a project of our own. The brief for that project finally came our way around three years ago, when Heather asked to meet me to discuss how to progress a new business that she had co-founded in the menopause space, something I knew little about.

When I met with Heather to talk about the business, I was faced with a more rounded, experienced, and mature individual, who – and this is something I have learned to recognise in the people I meet – had that glint in her eye that said she had found the thing that she was going to succeed with and that nothing would stop her. In short, a chance conversation between Heather and her friend Sam Simister about their battles with menopause had led the pair to conclude that there were scarce resources available to educate or help women through this inescapable, daunting, and mostly unchartered life stage. As is the case in many classic founder backstories, they wanted to do something to improve the situation.

## A light in the dark – and a plan

Heather and Sam invested their own money to commission a study into menopause, which led to the publication of *The Invisibility Report*.[10] To this day, the findings outlined in that document form the pivotal foundation upon which GenM has been built.

The report threw a spotlight on many issues, mainly that there are 15.5 million women in the UK alone who are going through menopause. Of those women, a huge percentage believe that brands could play a vital role in helping them with this – and Heather and Sam deserve all the credit for uncovering the forty-eight signs and symptoms of menopause. Not just those well-known ones that even men like me can cite, such as hot sweats, mood swings, and lack of libido, but forty-five others, some of which had never been directly linked with menopause before and could, I later discovered, be mistaken for signs or symptoms of life-threatening diseases like cancer. The impact of the misunderstanding, the lack of awareness, and the overall ignorance of society towards menopause was profound, and Heather and Sam decided to do something about it.

By the time I came in, they had spent somewhere between a year and eighteen months bringing their vision to life through an attempt to build a one-stop webshop. The site was going to stock products that could in some way, shape, or form help with one or more of the forty-eight symptoms they'd identified and target this significant demographic of menopausal

---

10. GenM, *The Invisibility Report* (GenM, 2020), https://gen-m.com/wp -content/uploads/2020/12/Generation-Menopause-The-Invisibility -Report.pdf, accessed November 2024

women who had an interest in or a need for those solutions.

It was far more than a crass commercial attempt to cash in on a market opportunity. I've never doubted that their integrity and desire to truly educate and bring light to a dark space were absolutely at the heart of everything they have done. As for my involvement, people like Heather Jackson don't come to see me because things are going well. They come because they aren't, or perhaps not as fast as they would like. It is in Heather's DNA to operate on a time scale that is from another dimension compared to most people in the business world, even those who profess to be highly productive and ambitious. Once she is on a mission, she eats, sleeps, and breathes it. Looking back, I can see that this webshop was never going to be built quickly enough for Heather, but for me, it wasn't just about speed. There were more fundamental weaknesses in their plan.

First, when I asked them how many people were in their team and what their budgets were, without giving away secrets, you could have multiplied those numbers by ten and, in my mind, they still wouldn't have had the capacity to build a truly thriving web store of the scale needed to make any impact. Second, there just weren't enough brands out there ready to be sold in the shop; very few had realised that the commercial opportunities related to menopause potentially presented them with their first chance to do something both truly purposeful and truly profitable. Another huge factor, of course, was that the women who needed to find the site wouldn't be looking for it, whether it was live or not, because they didn't know it existed. There were challenges on every front.

## A radical change in approach

I think Heather, to this day, feels some regret about the fact that they chose the wrong path in their first attempt to accomplish their mission, but two things need to be said about that.

First, most brands get it wrong on their first attempt. However you look at it, it takes ten years to build an overnight success, and, in that decade, many brands explored different routes from the one they fundamentally ended up taking.

Second, to me, Heather and Sam's idea was never to build a website. That was the route they chose, but their vision was simply to do the right thing by 15.5 million women by shining a spotlight on what had previously been a taboo area. Working with them, it became obvious to me and my team that there was an opportunity to fulfil that mission in a cleaner, more effective, and more achievable way to get the results that they craved but at a faster pace, using funding from far bigger organisations than ours. At the heart of that plan was the logic that if there's a marketplace of

15.5 million women, brands should be interested in it, and if GenM positioned itself as the conduit between those women and those brands, the brands could pay a membership fee for access to insight and intel relating to that hugely valuable market.

## A mark that means something – the MTick

Heather and the team acted quickly to build on the idea, starting with the creation of the MTick, which you can think of as the menopause equivalent of the Vegan V, which you will only find on true vegan products. GenM was going to become the home of the MTick, and our job at Propaganda would be to show brands the commercial value that 15.5 million women in the UK represented to them. We had a purposeful opportunity – that is, we had customers who needed help, and our task was simply to kickstart brands into giving it. But we also knew that we didn't want this to become something that was exploited by brands with no integrity that had no right to cash in on that space and push their products onto an already vulnerable market – not with our help, anyway. Thus, the MTick was launched as a genuine mark of integrity. It is a stamp of approval given, following a process that validates GenM members and shows that key criteria have been met – we have declined brands on many occasions for not meeting the required standard. Just like the Vegan V, the MTick on the corner of a menopause product is a sign of authenticity and gives consumers the confidence to know that it will serve them well.

## Driven by a powerhouse

Our team were constantly inspired and motivated by Heather Jackson's infectious nature. When I say that, I am certainly not decrying the pivotal role that Sam played, but while she was working hard on infrastructure and the essential rigour of the MTick – crossing all the Ts and dotting the Is in the background – there was the 'Duracell Bunny' (as I would affectionately call her) that is Heather Jackson. She shows little to no fear of anything and could just go out there and sell the GenM concept to the biggest of the big corporates as though it were child's play. She bows to no one when she's out in the field, and that's a superpower where talking to corporates is concerned, because she has always been able to face whoever is in front of her as an equal and earn their respect.

Still on the topic of Heather, something that I think is an important point to mention is that living under the shadow of a celebrity father must be hard for anybody. When I look at Heather, I often wonder how much of that pressure to succeed or to 'be someone' has resulted in her being who she is today. I must also tell her, via this book, that she should be in no doubt whatsoever of the impact on society and the good for humankind that her energy has created through the manifestation of her vision in GenM. Certainly, in my eyes, she's now the greater of the two celebrities in her family and I think the sooner she realises that, the better. This is intended as nothing other than an indirect but huge compliment to Ashley. However, there is no doubt in my mind that the true celebrity in terms of the legacy left is one Miss Heather Jackson.

GenM's coruscating rise to the forefront of this growing sector is inseparable from the growth of the sector itself. Not only did GenM manage to sit at the vanguard with the likes of Davina McCall and Dr Louise Newson, but it was responsible for generating buzz and celebrity interest. If it were not for GenM, with Heather driving it, I'm not sure whether the sector would have formed as quickly as it has.

The work we did to refocus how to articulate the GenM vision and realise it via a far more achievable yet larger channel than simply an online shop, and to redefine GenM's role as one that unites useful brands with 15.5 million women (and the commercial opportunities they present), has been incredible. That thinking demonstrated a great deal of strategic prowess on our part. Since then, our involvement has evolved into more of a regular branding consultancy role, and we are always trying to keep up with the rapid pace at which Heather wants to move.

I have deliberately referred to this process as us 'keeping up with' Heather because most of the time, we can confidently say that our job with any client is to create a brand that's a year ahead of the reality of the operation – the operation then grows to meet the vision, as we did with Clipper and ghd, for example.

It's been an underlying feature of every other piece of work we've done. Not so with GenM. I'd say that, at best, we've managed to keep pace with Heather's plans. She is instinctively ahead of the game in any area she applies her focus to, not just GenM, as that is how she ticks. As much as she likes all the work that we do, she has always wanted to be a year ahead of everything we've been able to throw at her, which makes for a sometimes-tense relationship where the challenges we face and the 'creative debates', as I will politely call them, can be difficult for the team. That's not a criticism of Heather or the team, but a reflection of how unique this project is. It is not like any other work we have done, and Heather is not like our other clients. Whereas clients are usually in awe of us because of the vision we can bring to the table, Heather is seeing stuff that no one else is – but until she found us, she struggled to find anyone who could understand her vision, let alone act on it and drive it forward.

## Setting an example – a beacon of light for other brands

We have to remind ourselves that we're not working on a normal brief here. This isn't just about generating profits to increase shareholder value for clients. This is truly an embodiment of purpose for profit, to a level I've never seen before. My main impression of GenM, and the way that I see the brand, is as a beacon to other organisations that want to make money while doing good. In that regard, GenM is an inspiration and a leader, pointing to a new commercial world where brands can no longer exist simply to sell sugar and make children fat. Founders need to go back to the drawing board and ask themselves how they can create stuff that benefits the world *and* makes them money, and I believe GenM is simply the world's best example of that to date.

From the point when I met Heather, when her vision was simply to build a product that offered information and signposting, through which we might somehow be able to build revenue from advertising fees – an idea we drew a line through early on – GenM has evolved into a much bigger membership organisation. Every member – and there are now well over a hundred – must pay a fee of anywhere from £5,000 to £50,000, depending on their size and scale.

I have lost count of the number of products that exist that are now carrying the MTick, and the same goes for the sheer volume of shelf space that is being given to menopause and where the GenM mark serves as crucial signposting. In short, GenM has created an entirely new retail category, and I am proud to have been a part of that journey, and to continue to be now as the organisation's chair. At times it has felt like it's been as difficult and intense as chairing my own business.

I have spoken a lot about Heather in this chapter, but as I mentioned before, GenM couldn't have happened without Sam, whose role was more operational and so could easily fly under the radar.

GenM is now 'The Menopause Partner for Brands' – an organisation leading other pioneering organisations in its quest to normalise the conversation and improve the menopause experience for all. Through GenM, brands can cater to women experiencing menopause – in business, to help raise the ethical commercial opportunity of serving a menopause audience, and externally to consumers, ensuring organisations commit to representing, educating, supporting, and portraying this audience in an authentic way.

There are two reasons why I was happy to step up as chair of GenM. First, I think Heather needs a great ally, a twenty-four-seven person as opposed to one who is only available between nine and five. I can provide that support because, like her, I don't follow the standard work rules or schedule, and most of our conversations are had in the hours when most people don't want them. Second, something happened early on in the life of GenM that made me want to join her and make the battle for better menopause somewhat part of my own life's purpose.

## The human cost of failing to understand menopause – Linda and David Salmon's story

I was deeply affected by a news piece I read about a man whose fifty-six-year-old wife took her own life.[11] They'd been together for forty-one years. Linda Salmon was experiencing intense feelings of anxiety linked to perimenopause and was eventually completely overwhelmed by them. Her husband, David Salmon, had had no idea what she was going through. He didn't know that anxiety and suicidal thoughts could be symptoms of menopause until after her death when he watched a television feature about the transition.

David said, 'I really thought the menopause was all about hot flushes. I didn't know anything about the invisible symptoms, particularly those associated with mental health,' which points to the lack of knowledge about menopause. He continued, 'We'd spoken to the doctor, and she was eventually diagnosed with anxiety, but they made no mention of the menopause or why this might have come about,' which mirrors Heather Jackson's experience: she had only understood what was happening to her after chatting with Sam. 'If we had properly understood what was going on and the symptoms Linda was experiencing,' David added,

---

11. BBC News, 'Menopause: Bereaved husband urges men to spot mental health signs' (BBC, 12 November 2021), www.bbc.co.uk /news/uk-england-leeds-59208883, accessed November 2024

'we'd have been able to get her the help she needed and she might still be here with us today,' highlighting the saddest part of this tragic story and why GenM's work is so important.

David and Linda's story shows that menopause doesn't just affect the women who experience it but all the people who care about them, including the men in their lives. This isn't a female-only issue. It affects all of society. Sadly, Linda wasn't the first woman to take such drastic action to end her suffering, and she won't be the last. Her story could just as easily have been Sam's or Heather's or even my wife's. Everyone has a breaking point. I hate the thought that someone I love could be struggling in that way, not understanding what was happening to them and, worse still, feeling unable to talk to others about it.

Through GenM, I feel a little better knowing that I am a part of the solution, and that makes this project one of my greatest achievements. Learning about the forty-eight signs and symptoms of menopause was also eye-opening, and I wanted to do something creative and memorable to share these with others, rather than presenting a list. So, I authored a poem to talk about them instead, which was a tougher mission than it might sound.

## An MCA award winner for social impact

Propaganda's work for GenM won an MCA award for social impact in 2022. This is one of many awards we have received from the MCA, with little competition from what other people would refer to as 'agencies'. We see business and brand transformation, which is what we're all about, far more often being done in the consulting world by organisations such as Deloitte or PwC than by design agencies. It never felt right for us to try and compete in any of our normal industry awards because first, I think the best work we have ever done would lose simply because the industry doesn't understand it; and second, most of the work we did fifteen years or more ago, which paradoxically would probably have gone and won awards from our industry, is not the work we feel most proud of. This just goes to show that, in short, most of these awards are judged and claim victory based on cheap visual puns. None of them dives into the substance and the balance sheet to understand whether a material impact has been made – with the exception of the MCA, and that's where I decided to play.

I have indulged myself a little by adding a page at the back of this book to show all of our MCA awards because I think it shows how Propaganda, a small company from Huddersfield now situated in Leeds – often cited as one of the branding capitals of the North – has gone on to create a space for branding where most other agencies have never dreamed of operating, namely the

C-suite. More than that, we can also compete on the world stage against the leviathans of consulting – and we can win. This is another thing we have in common with Heather Jackson – that neither of us bows down to anyone!

## TEN

# Visceralisation

A t the start of this book, I described the way that seeing a pitch invasion by Leeds United's VYT made me feel. At the end of that introduction, I threw out a question: what is brand? I hope you are now better equipped to answer that question for yourself. If *Brand Warfare* has given you a clearer perspective on this, my job is done.

## How to define brand

There are a thousand definitions out there, all failing to define brand at the level that interests me. All of them look at brand from an academic point of view, but the inherent problem is that they fail to consider it from the consumer's perspective, which is the most important thing. I work on the basis that brand is deeply personal and profoundly visceral. It's about how *you* feel. 'Visceral' can have two meanings:

1. Relating to the viscera

2. Relating to deep inner feelings rather than to intellect and logic

My responsibility as a brand builder is to *visceralise* a product, so that it penetrates the souls of the people it is meant for. *Visceralisation* is my process.

We visceralise products, taking them from being no more than bits of material pulled together to carry out a function, into items that some people love and others hate. I've said many times that our job has never been to make any of the brands we've worked for 'liked', which is a banal emotion. Visceralisation breathes life into machinery, vehicles, and tools. Organisations become more than bricks, mortar, and websites. They become cherished, respected, and, in the case of some that I have worked on, worshipped.

To understand a brand, you must go beyond the surface and consider experiences. These are tethered to emotional responses, feelings that are, at times, inexplicable. A brand, in its truest form, is a relationship, and it is a deeply intimate one.

A brand is also visceral because it gets under your skin. It becomes part of your identity. There's a reason why people wear certain logos with pride or feel impassioned about defending their preferred products. It's because these brands resonate on a level that transcends utility. They become part of who we are and how we see ourselves.

The centrality of this deeply personal connection means that the essence of a brand can't be universally defined. It's subjective and ever-changing. What one person loves, another might despise. And that's okay. It highlights the fluidity and complexity of what a brand truly is.

Marketing gurus can attempt to script every interaction, to make a brand feel a certain way, but they cannot dictate the personal experiences and emotions that people attach to it. Each consumer brings their own history, biases, dreams, and desires to the table. These elements intertwine to shape their unique perception of a brand.

So while traditional descriptions like 'a brand is a promise' or 'a brand is what people say about you when you're not in the room' have their place, they fall well short of capturing its essence. Yes, a brand can promise reliability, luxury, innovation, or kindness. And, yes, people will talk about it, critique it, and recommend it. But at its core, a brand lives inside us. It's a heartbeat, a visceral response, a deeply personal bond that defies simple categorisation.

In essence, a brand is a feeling, an experience, an unspoken connection between what it represents and the person who embraces that representation. It's not just seen or heard; it's felt, and the feeling it elicits is what makes a brand truly unforgettable.

For me, I felt this when I wore the Giorgio Armani eagle. I became fearless. When I work for other brands, I always strive to create just as intense a feeling between them and their customers.

## Become the customer

So how do we create this feeling? How do we build a brand? How do we *visceralise* a product?

Someone suggested that I share my ten commandments on branding. I didn't intend to author a how-to manual, but if we take my definition of brand as a starting point, the process of how to build a brand logically follows. Applying the principle of knowledge before assumption, I believe there is one primary commandment, from which everything else flows:

Thou shalt...become the customer.

Who uses your product or service? Understanding these people holds the key to every other door. However, it's not simply a case of gaining a detailed perspective *of* them. That's the cold, useless, academic approach. Knowing their age range, gender, hobbies, interests, vital statistics and favourite colours will point you to where they are and how to find them, but you must go beyond the fascia of research to get to the real juice.

You need to walk in their shoes. Become the customer.

To know them properly, to empathise with them, and know how things feel for them, you must become a 'method marketeer'. Just as the greatest actors – the likes of Robert De Niro, Marlon Brandon, Daniel Day-Lewis, and Heath Ledger – used a 'method acting' approach to become the characters they played, you must become the consumer you're trying to sell your brand to.

I could have written a list of three, ten, or one hundred branding commandments, but you *must* start with the customer. Shift the focus away from the product and what you think its value proposition is – its intended function – and discover what it means to the people who are loyal to it. To do that, you must become the customer so that you can understand them on a granular level, not just a statistical one. This approach is in the DNA of our planning teams and the central focus when they embark on Brand Discovery.

Once we know what it is to *be* the customer, nothing is guesswork. We have more than data. We have experience. We feel the emotions that drive their loyalty, and we become naturally fluent in the language of those emotions. This empowers us to build that all-important connection between the essence of a brand and the people who embrace it, and to lean into ideas that will get under their skin.

That's visceralisation, and it's the central idea upon which I built Propaganda and, in turn, went on to build brands, some of which you've read about in this book. Maybe visceralisation isn't for everyone. But then again, I've never been everyone!

# Epilogue: Life Equips You

Most of us, in job interviews or meetings with prospects, have been asked to talk about our 'experience', and the answer we're expected to give is a list of brands that have hired us, projects we've been involved with, and places we have worked. That's all good and relevant, but those responses don't fully answer the question. They form an important part of our journey but miss the essential element.

If someone asked me what experience I had, I'd start by saying, 'My own.' Whose experience do they need to hear about? If people are defined solely by their education and previous job roles, what's the point of interviewing them? Are two people with first-class degrees in biochemistry from Oxford University the same? If neither has a degree, should they both be equally disregarded? None of that is intended to sound flippant. Beyond the things typically mentioned, the experiences that carry the most value are the formative ones that we face throughout life and begin to affect us profoundly long before we start down a career path.

We are more than the sum of our qualifications, previous projects, and job roles. These formative experiences we have, which are not usually written on any application form or curriculum vitae, make us who we are and prepare and equip us for what we do later. We shouldn't be concerned about oversharing when speaking about the experiences that forged us. What is it that has shaped our views, style, ethos, and ethics – the parts of our character that were established long before we embarked on our commercial paths? I find the answers to these questions far more interesting than the usual responses when people are asked about their 'experience'.

While reflecting on my life in business, I have been struck by the realisation that Propaganda is the product of my personal rather than professional experiences – lessons I was learning without knowing I was learning. In the 1984 cult classic film, *The Karate Kid*,[12] Mr Miyagi doesn't openly teach 'Daniel San' how to kick, punch, and block. He asks him to wash the car and paint the fence, much to Daniel's frustration. There is a method in Miyagi's apparent madness: he is giving Daniel the muscle memory required for effective blocking. This

---

12. Avildsen, J G, *The Karate Kid*, Columbia Pictures (1984)

is a great example of how our experiences equip us for the things we don't even know we will be doing yet.

Life doesn't teach us transparently, either. We are not provided with a textbook, and learning is not linear. Learning for work, learning for being in business, learning for your career, learning for when you're on the payroll, doesn't start when you show up at the office on your first day, launch a company, or get your foot onto the first rung of your chosen career ladder.

I can point to various life experiences that, in hindsight, I can see equipped me for my career in branding. Some were passion pointers, showing me the way to a more fulfilling life. Others told me who I am. Some *made* me who I am. But none was given to me on a plate or spelled out. No manual was presented, and no guide said, 'Take this. It will serve you well. You are going to need it later.' It sounds clichéd, but you must listen to your gut and go where it is prodding you.

It is worth noting that, in some cultures, the gut is considered far more than a digestive organ. The Japanese, for example, refer to that region of the body as the *hara* and consider it to be a person's true centre, the base of the soul.[13] It is where the centre of gravity is in the human body, and it is here that a defeated samurai was expected to plunge his *tantō* (dagger) when carrying

---

13. O Ratti and A Westbrook, *Secrets of the Samurai: A survey of the martial arts of feudal Japan* (Tuttle, 1991)

out the ritual suicide known as *seppuku* (formal) or *hara-kiri* (common name), cutting through the abdomen from left to right. Perhaps the advice that we should listen to our gut isn't so clichéd after all.

The need to conform to expectations and fear of rejection, failure, or of not fitting in can all interfere with the messages that come from our souls. Instead of questioning where you are in life and looking elsewhere saying, 'If only' you had done that course, gained that qualification, or gone down that other path, why not consider the possibility that everything that was supposed to happen already has and – without you knowing – you've acquired characteristics, strengths, and approaches that will take you where you need to be. If the old adage, 'Everything happens for a reason' carries any validity, then this is it. It's pointless trying to become something you are not. Life has served you what you needed to move towards your destiny when you are ready to. You are equipped to do whatever you need to do. My life presents a perfect example of this.

From a young age, it was obvious that I was interested in art and graphic design, but I didn't understand why or how I would use those skills later in life. Drawing was something I did to express myself. Embracing the goth look was another form of self-expression, but I was still looking for my tribe.

My first encounter with casual culture took me one step closer to understanding what makes me tick. It was intoxicating, overwhelming, and all-consuming. I was in love from the first second, but what was I really attracted to, apart from the designer labels? It wasn't the violence, but everything else that came with it. What was violence in casual culture built on? It was built on loyalty and bravery in extremely daunting situations – situations that I could not only deal with but thrive in, because the fear was drowned out by excitement. There was also the feeling that we were standing up for something. I perceived Leeds as the underdogs. They were a team that had fallen from a pedestal and were struggling in the lower leagues, so there was a strong feeling that I was fighting for them in their time of need.

That drive to stand up for others has stayed with me throughout my career while working with clients who have found themselves in difficult situations, sometimes through failure, apathy, or poor decision-making but often because of circumstances beyond their control. Whenever they needed someone to give them the courage and strength to stand their ground, face whatever adversity they were up against, and mount a fightback, Propaganda has stood shoulder-to-shoulder with them.

I do have some red lines. To this day, I will not work with a brand that I can't throw my weight behind 100%. I have to be all in, and that means I have to be behind its values. No commercial opportunity, no amount of money or glory will persuade me to work with anyone who partakes in fox hunting, for example.

Others may judge me for the decisions I made over thirty years ago, but I'd argue that getting into football violence was part of the process of understanding what I was about. At the time, all I knew was that I wanted to be a part of it – the excitement, rebelliousness, and adrenaline of casual culture. Now I recognise that what I really wanted was camaraderie, a sense of belonging, a cause, and to be challenged.

For the first time, I knew exactly who I was and where I wanted to be. At least for that moment, I had found my tribe. It was also a time when I experienced first-hand the power of branding and an attraction to brand values. Even though I was unaware of it, my compulsion to join the NCL was a lesson in branding and its purpose. My job is to create that attraction and draw in the right people for the brands I work with. When someone walks into my office, wanting me to inject new life into their brand, the standard I have set myself is to transform it in such a way that its consumers feel the same visceral, irresistible pull as I did when I first donned an Armani sweatshirt, and to create a bond that defies logic and lasts for years.

My time with the casuals equipped me for life in business in many ways. No boardroom scenario could compare with some of the scary situations I had experienced as a dresser. That has given me the courage to speak out and stand up for what I believe in without fear of the consequences. Without that conviction, would I have embraced the planning methodology? Or would I have continued down the same route as everyone else, happy to take the money for doing what we were expected to do – even when we knew that the approach wouldn't deliver results?

The day I stood up to a dinosaur at IBM, a man who had made the company notorious for being an agency graveyard, the director took me on not because of the ideas I had presented – no matter how strong they were – but because they were attracted to me. They felt that they could trust me. When I stood up to the board member who was being overtly rude to me in that meeting, the director saw something much more powerful than anything I could put in a presentation. They saw something that you can't fake – authenticity. They saw my conviction, honesty, and courage and said to themselves, 'This is a guy we can work with. We can count on him to fight for our corner.' That's why I was hired. My behaviour, albeit completely unorthodox and unfitting of what is expected of a professional, was in complete alignment with my heart and values. The director saw my character.

Courage is a key part of my and Propaganda's journey. We set up with a shoestring budget and were deceived by a supplier on our first job, which had taken three months to win. That didn't stop us. We were the first agency outside of London to adopt the planning methodology, a massive risk. Imagine getting rid of the lion's share of your team and investing that money into a handful of planners. It was a huge gamble, but I believed it was the right thing to do, and it paid off.

That's another thing I learned as a casual: to do the right thing, even if my sense of what the 'right thing' was during my football warring days was misguided. When I started to sense that the VYT didn't stand for anything but violence and hooliganism, I turned my back on it. I am a warrior, not a bully or a thug. I was enamoured by the VYT brand when I first joined. They lost my support when they forgot their roots and their brand values. Another lesson.

A strong brand is irresistible. When a brand speaks to you, you will move mountains to get it – save up for weeks, liquidate a store card, work overtime, or, in my case, knit an Armani logo into another garment. Brands transcend functionality. They touch us in another, deeper way, and when they don't, we move on to something else.

When I was set up to fail by the printer I hired for my first contract, I learned one of my most important lessons: business is war. The same rules that I had learned on the terraces applied to the boardroom. One of these rules is the principle of quality over quantity. There were many occasions when my friends and I were outnumbered and still came out of situations on top, or we saw other small groups holding their own against much bigger firms. If the underdog can win in such a physically demanding arena – literally outweighed in a game that's all about strength, muscle, and endurance – surely the same applies to other environments, where those with the best ideas will achieve victory.

We applied that principle to our recruitment policy from the very beginning, only taking on the best talent from the industry. And the recruitment process was designed to test the mettle of candidates beyond their on-paper credentials. It takes a special kind of individual to accept the gauntlet that we threw at them – 'Well done. You're hired. You've got three months to prove yourself' – especially when the word was out that we weren't joking, and that many didn't make it. I demanded a real response to the question, 'What experience do you have?' I wanted to find people with true grit, determination, unique talent, and character.

When I was working as an apprentice for a screen printer, I was tasked with keeping the floor clean. It may not seem like rocket science, but keeping our environment clean and tidy is important, and someone has to do it. That person should be anyone who spots an issue. Even now, if I notice litter on the floor, I pick it up, and I expect others to do the same because it is everyone's responsibility. If they don't, that says a lot about them – 'not my job,' 'not my responsibility,' 'I'm better than that,' or 'that's beneath my pay grade' – and none of it is good. Sometimes the small things prove to be far more telling than the big things. If someone has a stinking attitude towards something as simple as taking care of the environment they are working in, how will that affect their behaviour in other areas? You can call me picky, but character sometimes counts for more than raw talent. You can teach someone new skills, but changing attitudes is more difficult.

It is now obvious to me that life was equipping me for launching and growing Propaganda. The terraces were replaced with the boardroom, and my loyalty is now to the brands I serve rather than a football club or its crew of casuals. This is not unique to me; life equips us all to find and walk our own paths. In fact, I am so convinced that this is the case, that I did a little research to see if there is a name for it, like the Japanese *ikigai*, which translates as 'purpose'. None of the results I found carried the same weight as *ikigai* in the sense that they hadn't become buzzwords used globally, but they were all still cool.

The German word *Lebenserfahrung* roughly translates to 'experience through life' and implies that the experiences we gain throughout life contribute to our skills, wisdom, and preparedness for future challenges. The Swedes have a similar word, *livserfarenhet*. The Japanese use the word *keiken* to mean experience in the sense that what we go through serves as a form of preparation to equip us for future events.

It seems, then, that the importance of experience in shaping and preparing us for the life ahead of us is appreciated throughout the globe.

If I had to pick a winner, it would be *keiken*. I'm in the business of brand warfare. That's what life has equipped me for. That's where my *keiken* took me. My parting wish is for you to identify the lessons that have shown you who you are and where you should be going. Are you doing what life has equipped you to do? If not, why not? What's stopping you?

# Appendix: Awards

Propaganda's work and people have been recognised by the Management Consultancies Association (MCA) since 2005.

The MCA is the representative body for management consultancy firms, and I am proud to say that Propaganda is the organisation's only brand consultancy. The association recognises our approach, which bridges business strategy with brand creativity, and membership is a badge of quality and efficacy.

I am immensely proud of the work we do at Propaganda and delighted to present our MCA awards in the order in which we won them.

| Year | Client | Award |
|------|--------|-------|
| 2005 | ghd | Business Strategy |
| 2006 | Spear & Jackson | Marketing |
| 2006 | Spear & Jackson | Innovation |
| 2007 | FMG | Marketing |
| 2007 | Propaganda | Consultant of the Year |
| 2008 | The Car People | Marketing |
| 2009 | Propaganda | Consultant of the Year |
| 2009 | Seabrook | Customer Engagement |
| 2009 | Propaganda | Best Small Firm |
| 2010 | Illamasqua | Customer Engagement |
| 2011 | BOOST | Customer Engagement |
| 2012 | Clipper | Customer Engagement |
| 2014 | FMG | Strategy |
| 2015 | Propaganda | Young Consultant of the Year |
| 2016 | The Car People | Customer Engagement |
| 2017 | ReGrow | Innovation |
| 2018 | ReGrow | Strategy |
| 2021 | Roberts | Support to a Client During COVID-19 |
| 2022 | GenM | Social Impact |
| 2023 | BSW Group | Strategy |

# Acknowledgements

It would be impossible to acknowledge everyone who has played a part in my journey from the terraces to the boardroom. I have worked with too many staff and clients over the course of thirty-three years to mention them all. Equally, it would be just as impossible to attempt to single out those friends that I made within the football casual community. In short, you know who you are.

What I can do is say thank you to my wife, children and of course my mum, dad and sisters. I must also thank my current board of directors at Propaganda – Laura, Craig, Bruce, Richard, James and Lee – as well as my PA, Joanne, who has been with me for eighteen years.

There are those who took the time to read drafts of the book in its formative stages, and I would specifically like to thank Susan Kenyon, Jonathan Hooley, Steve Murphy, Luke Walwyn, Paul Heywood, Lee Roberts, Ian Dickinson, Ian Spence, Max, Willetts, Steve Bailey, Chink, Richard Mitchie, Jay Lomax, Mark Evans and, of course, Martin Morrison, who helped shape my words.

# The Author

 Julian Kynaston is an
award-winning market-
ing leader and founder of
Propaganda, the pioneering
brand consultancy accredited
by the Management Con-
sultancy Association. With
over thirty years of experience, Julian has driven trans-
formative results for clients,
founded the iconic Illamasqua brand and helped scale
ghd to global success.

🌐 www.propaganda.co.uk

in www.linkedin.com/in/julian-kynaston